THE ROUGH GUIDE TO
Saxophone

**Whether you're a beginner or a pro,
whether you are about to buy a saxophone
or you want to learn more about the one
you already have – this book is for you**

Hugo Pinksterboer

THE ESSENTIAL TIPBOOK

Publishing Details

This first edition published September 2000 by Rough Guides Ltd,
62–70 Shorts Gardens, London WC2H 9AB

Distributed by the Penguin Group:
Penguin Books Ltd, 27 Wrights Lane, London W8 5TZ
Penguin Putnam, Inc., 375 Hudson Street, New York, NY 10014
Penguin Books Australia Ltd, 487 Maroondah Highway, PO Box
257, Ringwood, Victoria 3134, Australia
Penguin Books Canada Ltd, 10 Alcorn Avenue, Toronto, Ontario,
Canada M4V 1E4
Penguin Books (NZ) Ltd, 182–190 Wairau Road, Auckland 10,
New Zealand

Typeset in Glasgow and Minion to an original design by
The Tipbook Company bv

Printed in The Netherlands by Hentenaar Boek bv, Nieuwegein

© The Tipbook Company bv, 2000

128pp

A catalogue record for this book is available from the British
Library.
1-85828-649-2

THE ROUGH GUIDE TO
Saxophone

Written by

Hugo Pinksterboer

ROUGH
GUIDES

THE ESSENTIAL TIPBOOK

Rough Guide Tipbook Credits

Journalist, writer and musician **Hugo Pinksterboer** has written hundreds of articles and reviews for international music magazines. He is the author of the reference work for cymbals (*The Cymbal Book*, Hal Leonard, US) and has written and developed a wide variety of musical manuals and courses.

Illustrator, designer and musician **Gijs Bierenbroodspot** has worked as an art director in magazines and advertising. While searching in vain for information about saxophone mouthpieces he came up with the idea for this series of books on music and musical instruments. Since then, he has created the layout and the illustrations for all of the books.

Acknowledgements

Concept, design and illustrations: Gijs Bierenbroodspot

Translation: MdJ Copy & Translation

Editor: Kim Burton

IN BRIEF

Have you just started playing the saxophone? Are you thinking about buying a sax? Or do you want to know more about the instrument you already own? Then this book will tell you everything that really matters. You'll read about the names of all the parts, about lessons and practising. There are tips about what you should look and listen for when purchasing a sax or choosing a mouthpiece, what kind of reed to use, how to keep your instrument in top condition, and more.

A good choice
Having read this Tipbook, you'll be able to get the best out of your saxophone, buy the best instrument you can, and understand other literature on the subject, from books to catalogues and Internet publications.

Begin at the beginning
If you have just started playing, or haven't yet begun, pay particular attention to the first four chapters. If you've been playing any longer, you can skip ahead to chapter 5.

Glossary
The glossary at the end of the book briefly explains most of the terms you'll come across as a saxophonist and it doubles as an index.

CONTENTS

1. A SAXOPHONIST

Feel like whispering? Cackling, hissing, screaming? You might even want to talk. With a saxophone, you can do it all. And since the instrument can also play straightforward melodies, sax players are welcome in all sorts of bands, ensembles and orchestras. This chapter covers the role of the sax, the various members of the saxophone family, and what singers and saxophonists have in common.

With a saxophone you can play jazz or funk, classical, Latin, or rock and soul. In some styles – jazz, for example – you'll be expected to play a good number of solos. In other groups, you may find yourself in the middle of a saxophone section, adding spicy riffs or mellow colours to the music.

But can I play Mozart?

Saxophones are used in classical orchestras and concert bands too, but you won't come across them in music by Mozart or Beethoven; these classical composers died before Adolphe Sax invented the instrument around 1840.

Take a break

One important difference between playing the saxophone and playing, say, drums, guitar or bass, is that in most groups the sax doesn't play all the time. You get a lot of breaks while on stage – just like anybody else who plays a wind instrument.

Alto, tenor, soprano and baritone

Saxophones come in a whole array of sizes or *voices*. The alto sax and the lower-sounding tenor sax are the most

1

common, since their sound easily fits all kinds of music, and because they're a bit easier to master then the small, high-pitched soprano sax or the big, deep-sounding baritone.

Even higher, even lower
These four are not the only saxophones. There's also a sopranino, a bass and a rare contrabass.

Although they differ in appearance, all saxophones are basically the same instrument, with the same arrangement of keys. They just come in different sizes.

A tenor and an alto saxophone

A good ear
Saxophone playing is often compared with singing because you can do nearly as much on a sax as you can with your voice, and because, to be honest, you can play out of tune almost as easily as you can sing out of tune. When you strike a key on a piano, the note comes out in tune every time. On a sax, it can easily be a bit too high (*sharp*) or too low (*flat*). So learning to play the instrument well means developing a good ear.

Men only?
Are all sax players men? Taking a quick look around, you might say 'yes'. But there are well established female saxophonists as well, and many more are beginning to make their names. The Dutch Candy Dulfer is one prominent player, and there are also jazz players Ira Jane Bloom and, from England, Kathy Stobart and Barbara Thompson.

2. A QUICK TOUR

If you were to take a saxophone completely apart, you would end up with about two hundred bits and pieces comprising the body, the crook, the mouthpiece, the reed, and the key system with its numerous keys, pads, rods, pins, springs, corks and felts. Here's an introduction to the main parts of the sax: what they are, what they do and where to find them.

If you've never laid eyes on a sax before, it can appear a complicated piece of machinery. And it is. The point of all these parts, however, is to make playing the sax as easy as possible. Easier than a trumpet, for example, which looks deceptively simple. A sax, though, is basically just a long tube pierced by holes which can be closed or opened by the keys. The greater the number of closed holes, the lower the pitch of the sound. It's that simple.

They're all the same
Each saxophone has the same basic set of parts, whether it's a soprano, an alto, a tenor, or a baritone. In chapter 3, *Four*

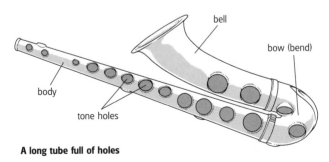

A long tube full of holes

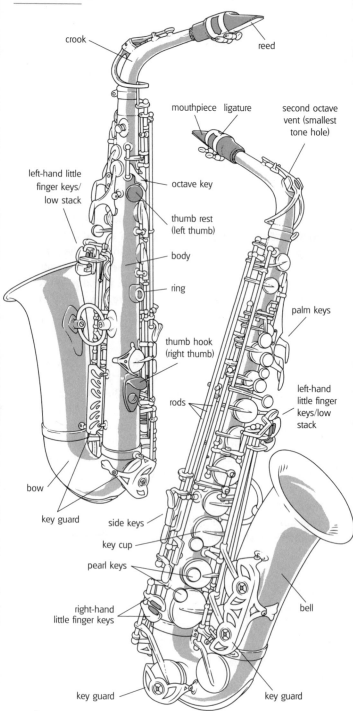

crook

reed

mouthpiece   ligature

second octave vent (smallest tone hole)

left-hand little finger keys/ low stack

octave key

thumb rest (left thumb)

body

ring

palm keys

thumb hook (right thumb)

left-hand little finger keys/low stack

rods

bow

key guard

side keys

key cup

pearl keys

right-hand little finger keys

bell

key guard

key guard

Saxes, you'll read everything about the differences between these four main instruments. The illustration on page 7 shows an alto.

The sound
When you sing your vocal chords vibrate, setting the air in motion and creating a sound. When playing the sax, you make the *reed* vibrate. This thin piece of cane is attached to the *mouthpiece* with a *ligature*. The body of the saxophone amplifies the sound and gives it its specific character.

Longer = lower
If you put a reed on the mouthpiece and blow it, all you get is a high-pitched squeal. Add the *crook* to the mouthpiece and the sound will be slightly lower and fuller. Put the *crook* onto the body of the sax and the pitch will go down even further. The longer the tube, the lower the pitch.

Tone holes
The body of a very basic flute such as a recorder is drilled with a line of holes, called *tone holes*. It's similar with the saxophone. And just as on the recorder, the lowest note on the sax will sound when all these holes are closed.

Keys
On a recorder you close the holes with your fingers. A saxophone has some twenty-five *keys* to do that for you, as most tone holes are not only too big to be covered by your fingers, they're also too far apart.

Pads
In order for a sax to play properly the tone holes need to be fully closed, without any air leaks. Therefore, the *key cups* that cover the tone holes are fitted with *pads*: small thin felt discs with a thin outer layer of leather.

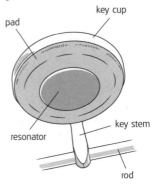

Resonators
In the middle of each pad you'll find a small metal or plastic

disc. These *resonators* make the sound of the sax a little brighter and more direct.

Wider and wider
The *body* of the sax becomes wider as it progresses from the crook to the bell; it has a *conical* bore. The tone holes at the top of the body are smaller than those at the bottom near the bell.

The smallest tone hole is on the crook: the *crook octave vent* or *upper octave vent*. The largest tone hole is located at the opposite end of the horn, in the bell.

Remote control
The forest of rods allows you to operate some twenty-five keys with only eight fingers and one thumb. It's somewhat like an old-fashioned remote control system; if you push something here, something somewhere else will move.

Springs
When you're not playing, about half of the keys are open; the others are closed. A series of needle-like springs make the key cups open or close when the keys are pressed. Some of these springs are illustrated on page 110.

Felts and corks
A number of felts and corks help keep the action quiet. They also help some keys open and close simultaneously, and determine how far some of the keys open.

Key guards
The easily damaged rods and key cups get some protection from a couple of *key guards*, which also keep your clothes from getting tangled in the action.

All thumbs
Your right thumb, under the *thumb hook*, supports the instrument. Your left thumb, placed on the *thumb rest*, operates the *octave key*.

Support
A neck strap or sling avoids you having to support the instrument with your fingers. The *ring* or *eye* for its hook is located about halfway up the body.

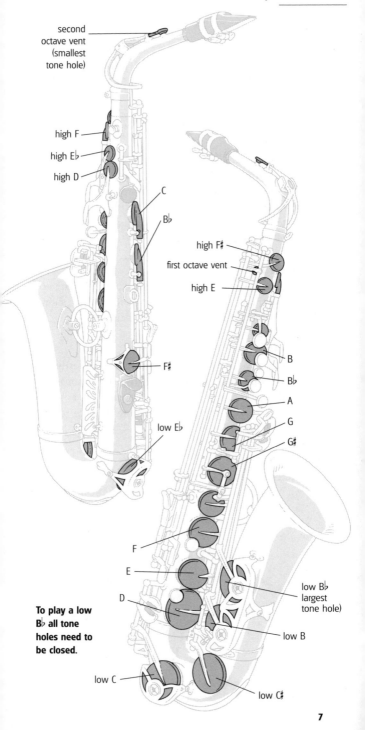

second octave vent (smallest tone hole)

high F
high E♭
high D

C
B♭

high F♯
first octave vent
high E

B
B♭
A
G
G♯

F♯

low E♭

F
E
D

low B♭ largest tone hole)

low B

To play a low B♭ all tone holes need to be closed.

low C

low C♯

7

THE KEYS

The keys of a saxophone have a variety of names. What one player calls a pearl key is a finger pad to the next, and catalogues and books may vary their terminology quite as much. Here's a brief introduction, so you know what's being talked about.

Keys and more

Technically speaking, keys are the things you press to open or close a tone hole. And the *key cups* are the things that actually cover the holes. When you press the octave key, you are actually opening one of the two key cups that are connected to it, but you'll find that many sax players use the word *key* for both.

A clear view

The illustrations on page 4 show the most important parts of the saxophone: the tone holes and their notes are shown on page 7, and the keys and levers on page 10.

Mother-of-pearl

Most saxes have eight keys operated by the fingertips on round 'buttons' inlaid with mother-of-pearl, or an imitation of that rather expensive material. *Pearl keys, key pearls, pearls* and, yes, *keys* are among the names used to refer to them.

The little fingers

Your left little finger controls four different keys. It takes quite a bit of practice to do this fluently in the beginning,

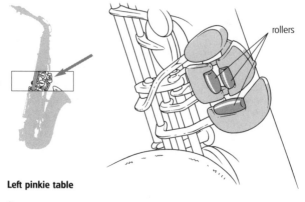

rollers

Left pinkie table

because to operate these *little finger* or *pinkie keys* requires quite a bit of strength in the weakest finger. The group of four keys is known as the *left little finger* or *pinkie table* or the *plateau*. The right little finger controls two similar keys. *Rollers* make it a little easier to slide from key to key.

Side and palm keys
You play the four or five *side keys* on the right-hand side with the inside of your fingers. On the left-hand side, there are three *palm keys* – played by the palm of your hand or the inside of the fingers. These two sets of keys are mostly used for playing high notes and trills.

Spatulas, levers, rockers and plates?
Owing to their spoon-like shape the front F, side and palm keys are sometimes referred to as *spatula keys* or *spatulas*. You may find that some players refer to certain keys as *levers*, such as the side C lever, operated by the right hand. And the *left hand floating rocker table* is another name for the four *touch plates* that are known as the left little finger table or the plateau.

NAMING THE KEYS
On a piano each note has its own key. That is not the case for the saxophone: for most notes you need a combination of keys. It follows that assigning note names to the keys isn't always straightforward. The simplest case of all is middle C-sharp, because you play that note without touching any keys at all. Sax players appropriately call this note *open C-sharp* (*open C♯*).

Naming systems
It is important to be able to identify each key, and a number of systems have been developed for the purpose. One of the most common, invented by the French saxophonist Jean Marie Londeix, is pictured on the following page.

Keys 1 to 6
When you hold a saxophone, your fingers should rest on keys 1 to 6. If you press key 1 only, you play the note B. Using keys 1 and 2 together, you get an A, and with keys 1, 2 and 3 together you get a G.

Key names according to the system of Jean Marie Londeix. The illustration shows an alto saxophone.

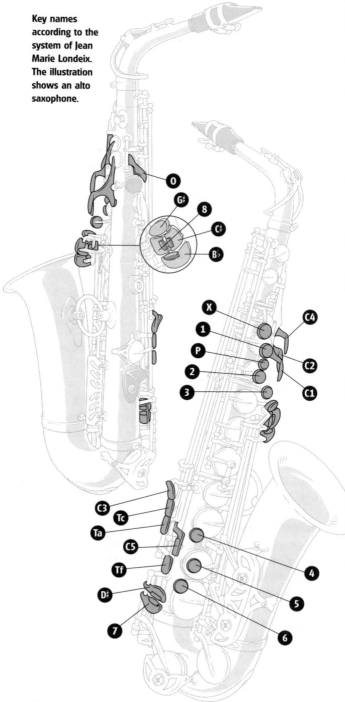

The little fingers

The right little finger operates key 7 (for the low C) and the key for the low E-flat (E♭). Pressing key 8, on the lower plateau, gives a low B. The names of the notes produced by using the other keys are shown in the illustration.

The octave key

Key O, on the back, is the *octave key*, also known as the *register key* or *octave lever*. With this key you open either one of the two octave vents, raising your note by one octave. The first octave vent is located between high E and high F-sharp (F♯), the second (upper) one is on the crook.

The highest notes

Keys C1 through C5 are for the very highest notes on the sax, and the higher the number, the higher the pitch. C5 is the high F♯. The keys named with a T are used to make playing trills simpler, although they also provide alternative fingerings for use in tricky passages. For example, the Tc key is used to play the note C. As for the trill keys:
• With Tc you can trill between B and C.
• With Tf you can trill between F and F♯.
• With Ta you can trill between A and B♭.

F = X

Key X, known as *front F*, *quick F* or *forked F*, is used to reach not only high F, but also high E and F♯ in certain passages.

Fingering chart

Most saxophone books include a fingering chart, showing you exactly which combination(s) of keys are used to play any given note. You will notice that some notes can be obtained with more than one fingering.

Low, middle and upper

Some saxophonists divide the range of the instrument into three registers: low, middle and upper. All the notes played without the octave key belong to the low register. Once you use the octave key, you are in the middle register and using the side and palm keys reaches the upper register.

Fingering chart.
Pressing the two
shaded keys
gives the note A.

11

3. FOUR SAXES

The four most popular saxophones are the soprano, the alto, the tenor and the baritone. This chapter tells all about their differences, their sound and their ranges – and it explains why a C is not always a C.

From a distance, you might say that a baritone sax looks nothing at all like a soprano sax. However, in terms of the mechanism and fingering they are basically the same. The baritone is just bigger, and thus lower in pitch. To make it manageable, it has been given some extra bends; if not, it would be over seven feet (more than two metres) long. The alto and the tenor lie between these two in size and pitch.

SOPRANO

At first sight the soprano sax resembles a clarinet, but a closer look reveals it to be quite a different instrument. The body of a clarinet is cylindrical except for a small bell at the end, and it's made of wood. The soprano sax, like its brothers, has a metal body that gets wider throughout its length, and it sounds very different. More metallic, some say, less woody or more piercing. Kenny G and Branford Marsalis, who's featured on several CDs by Sting, are well-known soprano players.

A soprano takes time

The soprano is not the easiest sax to play; it's harder to keep in tune than an alto or a tenor, and acquiring a good tone takes time and practise.

Soprano saxophone

Alto saxophone

ALTO

The alto sax is a good choice for a first instrument. It's at home in pretty much any style of music, and there's more classical music written for the alto than for any of the other saxes. It also plays an important role in concert and marching bands.

Well known players

David Sanborn and Phil Woods are two well-known alto saxophonists, and the late Charlie Parker is one of the most important saxophonists ever to play jazz. To get an idea of the sound of an alto in a symphony orchestra, listen to *The Old Castle* in Ravel's orchestration of Mussorgsky's *Pictures at an Exhibition.* Or check out recordings of classical soloists like John Harle, Fred Hemke and Jean-Yves Formeau.

TENOR

Many jazz musicians use the tenor sax as their main instrument, though you'll find it in other styles as well. Its sound might be described as fatter, juicier, richer or sexier than that of an alto or a soprano. The tenor can also be a good choice for the beginner, although the smaller and lighter alto is easier to handle.

The sound

The sound of a tenor is extremely versatile, ranging from a sturdy honk to an intimate purr. If you listen to the late Ben Webster or to Charles Lloyd you'll be treated to a soft, sensual tenor sound, while players like Michael Brecker,

Tenor saxophone

Baritone saxophone

Stanley Turrentine, Bob Berg or the late John Coltrane often sound more powerful, muscular, or even aggressive.

BARITONE

The baritone sax, with its looped crook, is the largest of the four, sounding an octave lower than the alto. It's not an ideal instrument for the beginner, as it's both unwieldy and expensive. Baritones are mainly used in big bands and concert bands. Without doubt the best-known baritone player is still the late Gerry Mulligan, who can be heard on many recordings. Two other well-known players are Ronnie Cuber and Pepper Adams.

HOW HIGH, HOW LOW?

If you have a keyboard, you can easily compare the range of the various saxes. The normal range of a sax is about two and a half octaves. Good players can stretch it to three or four octaves, or even further.

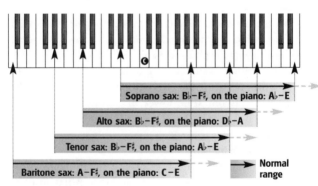

Soprano sax: B♭–F♯, on the piano: A♭–E
Alto sax: B♭–F♯, on the piano: D♭–A
Tenor sax: B♭–F♯, on the piano: A♭–E
Baritone sax: A–F♯, on the piano: C–E

Normal range

TRANSPOSING INSTRUMENTS

When you play a C on a piano or a guitar, you hear the note C. It's not the same thing on the saxophone; if you finger a C, you will *not* hear a C. Interested? Then read on. If not, skip to the next chapter.

Concert instruments

Pianos, guitars and many other instruments are in C. They are called *concert instruments*, because they sound in *concert pitch*: the note you play is the note you hear.

E-flat

Saxophones are *transposing instruments*. The alto and the baritone are pitched in E-flat. When you finger a C (press key 2 only), an E-flat is the note that you'll hear. That sounding note is called either *sounding E-flat* or *concert E-flat*.

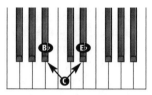

Fingering a C on the tenor sax sounds a concert B♭. A C on the alto sax sounds a concert E♭.

B-flat

The tenor and the soprano are in B-flat. Fingering a C (pressing the same key 2) results in a *concert B-flat*.

Confusing?

All of this sounds more confusing than it really is. You just finger the notes that you read, and the pitch that results is the one the composer wanted. If you don't read then you don't have to bother at all.

Transposed parts

Parts for saxophone players are *transposed parts*; they don't tell you which pitches to play, but which notes to finger. If you're playing the alto and a concert E-flat is required, a C will be written. If the same concert E-flat is supposed to be played on a tenor, then the written note will be an F; the tenor sounds one tone lower than concert pitch (a C sounds a B-flat, so an F sounds an E-flat).

Other wind instruments

Saxes are not the only transposing instruments. Most trumpets and clarinets, for example, are in B-flat, just like the soprano and tenor saxophones.

But why?

You could wonder why saxophones aren't just made in concert pitch. There are several reasons. First, a baritone sounds an octave lower than the alto because it's twice as long. So far there's no problem. But if these two instruments were to be made in C, then the tenor couldn't possibly also be in C as it's exactly halfway between the first two in length. That would mean it would have to be in F-sharp. Second, as said before, every sax has its own timbre, and this has a lot to do with its size. The size is what defines the pitch of the instrument. Most important, since there is a standard fingering which is the same for each instrument you can play both alto and tenor without having to learn two separate fingerings, since all the hard work of transposition is done for you when the part is written. Saxophones in C do exist, but they are very unusual nowadays (see page 93).

But why B-flat?

There are specific historical reasons for the use of transposing instruments, but they are rather involved. Any decent book on orchestration or instrumentation will give the full story if you are interested.

4. LEARNING TO PLAY

It doesn't take long to get a note out of the saxophone, but it takes plenty of time to learn how to play it well. Time and a good teacher. Playing the sax is rather different from simply blowing into it, as you'll soon see if you try. You may run out of breath, you'll probably find that your tone may be acceptable but not impressive, you may hear more squeaks than you'd like, and you may have difficulty staying in tune. This chapter focuses on learning how to play as well as you can.

There are quite a few sax players around, even professionals, who are mainly or completely self-taught. Still, a teacher may keep you from reinventing a variety of wheels as well as from developing bad habits and will teach you some good ones instead. Very importantly, any wind instrument teacher will be able to give proper guidance on breath control and embouchure, and unlearning poor air stream control and embouchure takes much more time than learning them properly in the first place. A good teacher may even be able to get you ready to hit the stage within a few months or a year.

Breath control

To be able to play long phrases, in tune and with a good tone, you need to develop proper breath and air stream control. Playing the saxophone is a lot more than simply blowing a lot of air into a mouthpiece. If you try to play a long, sustained note the first time you pick up a sax you'll probably feel dizzy and light-headed. Learning how to control your breath will cure this problem.

Embouchure

You also need a good *embouchure*. Saxophone player use this word (derived from the French 'bouche', meaning mouth) to describe the position and the use of lips, tongue, and the muscles of the face. Imagine how differently your speech sounds when you have a sore lip, or you try to speak without using your tongue. The embouchure has a vital influence on the sound of the saxophone.

Reading music

Do sax players need to be able to read music? You can get by without it – there are plenty of musicians who did, and still do – but reading music is a sure-fire way to get ahead on any instrument. It enables you to jam with others without first having to learn the music by heart, it allows you to use any of the hundreds of music books in print, to write down your own exercises or to jot down other players' parts. Also, the ability to read music can give you a better idea of what you're doing, which may help to make you a better player. Learning to read isn't such a daunting task as it might appear, either. It just needs a bit of determination and application.

Private teachers

There are thousands of private saxophone teachers if you do decide you need one. Expect to pay a professional teacher between £20–40/$30–50 per hour.

Questions, questions

On your first visit to a teacher, don't simply ask how much it costs. Here are a few tips.
- Can you take an introductory lesson? Then you can see if it clicks between you and the teacher. Or, for that matter, between you and the sax.
- Will you be taken on as a student if you are just learning for the fun of it, or are you expected to play for at least three hours a day?
- Do you have to invest in method books right away, or is course material included?
- Does the teacher have instructional videos, and can you borrow them?
- Can you record the lessons, so that you can listen at home to how you sound and to what was said during the lesson?

- Are you allowed to concentrate on the kind of music you want to play, or will you be required to learn other styles? Or will you be encouraged to do so?
- Is this teacher going to make you practice scales for two years, or will you be pushed on stage as soon as possible?
- Will the teacher give you advice on purchasing an instrument and other equipment?

Locating a teacher

Music shops may have a list of private teachers they can refer you to, or you could ask the Musicians' Union, which has a teachers' register. Some players have found great teachers simply by asking performers that they heard at a concert. Check the classified ads in newspapers, in music magazines or on supermarket bulletin boards, or pick up a copy of the *Yellow Pages*.

Collectives

You also may want to check whether there are any teachers' collectives or music schools in your vicinity. These may be able to offer such extras as ensemble playing, master classes and clinics.

PRACTICE

It is just as easy to play a low note on the piano or guitar as it is to play a high one. With the sax, however, it's not quite as simple. The lowest notes are awkward for a beginner, and it'll be a while before you get the highest notes out clearly. It can take six months, a year, or more, but eventually the notes will come.

Half an hour a day

Whichever instrument you play, you are better off practising for half an hour each day than for an entire afternoon once a week. This is particularly important in the case of wind instruments: you are not going to be able to develop your embouchure and air stream control if you only pick up the instrument once every seven days.

Your sound

It's your sound rather than how high or how fast you can play that makes the first impression on a listener. That's good news, as working on your sound makes a lot of other things fall into place as well. A good sound requires a well-developed embouchure and decent air stream control, which in turn helps you play in tune. Eventually you'll develop the control you need to create a whole range of sounds from fat to sweet, shrill to throaty, and ultimately you'll find your own personal sound. It's very helpful to record your practice sessions, as listening to the playback can give you a good idea of what your sound is really like and the areas you need to work on.

And your ears
On a sax you are the one responsible for getting the notes in tune, just as you are when you sing. Practising also involves training your ears, and learning how to pitch each note properly in tune. The more you play, the better you should be able to tell whether you're in tune or not.

THE NEIGHBOURS
It's considerably more difficult to play a sax softly than to play it at full volume. Beginners often make a lot of noise, and not always with the sweetest tone. If you are worried about disturbing your family or neighbours, the best thing to do is to soundproof a large cupboard, the corner of a room, or a part of an attic or a basement. As a sax player, you don't need much space to practice.

Mutes, towels and bags
If building a practice space is impractical, then a saxophone mute is a lot simpler and cheaper. It's a padded ring that you insert into the bell of your horn to reduce the volume. An ordinary hand towel may work just as well, but both solutions have their disadvantages, as they make the lowest notes difficult to produce and it is much harder to work on getting a good tone. It's also possible to get a bag that completely covers the instrument, considerably cutting down the volume. All the same, if playing at home does cause problems, the best solution is to find somewhere nearby where you can make as much noise as you need to.

Your own ears
If you are playing in a heavily amplified band, or if you're

practising at full volume in a small space, it doesn't hurt to consider your own ears. Even the most basic foam rubber earplugs will prevent ringing ears or other hearing damage. Of course, there are more sophisticated versions as well, available at music shops and chemists. The most luxurious protectors are custom made to fit your ears and have adjustable or replaceable filters.

GETTING BETTER

To conclude this chapter, here are a few more tips on practice technique. Practising can be a lot more fun using play-along cassettes and CDs which are available for practically any style of music, and a lot of music books these days come with tapes or discs of examples to illustrate points in the text.

Keeping time

Remember: drummers aren't the only ones who have to be able to keep time – saxophonists have to, as well. It's good to practice with a metronome, at least once in a while. This small device ticks or beeps out a steady adjustable pulse, helping you to work at keeping a regular tempo, timing and rhythm.

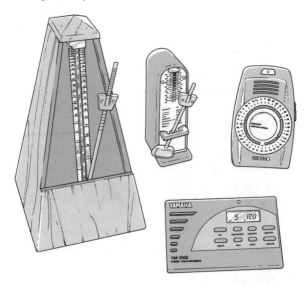

Two mechanical (wind-up) metronomes and two electronic ones

Electronics and computers

A drum machine can be a useful alternative to the metronome. There are similar machines that can be programmed to play bass lines and simple harmonies too, and even machines as well as software programs that offer you an entire band to play along to. *Phrase trainers* are devices that can slow down a musical phrase from a CD or other source to help you figure out even the meanest and fastest licks (as jazz musicians call phrases) at your own speed. There is also a computer that can do the same thing.

And finally

The two best ways to learn how to play? Play as much as you can, whether alone or in a band, and go out to see other musicians play. Whether they are living legends or local amateurs, you can learn something from every gig.

5. BUYING A SAX

A saxophone is not a cheap instrument, and a saxophone suitable for a beginner can easily cost four times as much as a beginner's guitar. Why the difference, and how much does it cost to play the saxophone? This chapter tells you what you need to know before you go out shopping for a horn. How to go about actually selecting an instrument is the main subject of chapter 6, *A Good Sax.*

A new entry-level alto or tenor sax can easily cost around £500/$750. Why so much? It's mainly because, with all the small and intricate parts that are involved, the making of a sax is a labour-intensive and time-consuming affair. Professional instruments start at around £1600/$2000, and may cost more than twice as much.

Baritones and sopranos
Baritones cost more, not just because they're bigger, but also because there are fewer of them made than there are altos and tenors. Conversely, a soprano may cost more than an alto or a tenor of comparable quality because its small size makes it more difficult to manufacture an instrument that plays both well and in tune. In turn, a relatively cheap baritone may sound quite good, since it's that little bit easier to get the low register in tune.

Pro horns for beginners
A great saxophonist can sound great on an inexpensive instrument, while beginning players would be much better off with professional quality horns; the latter are easier to play, and easier to play in tune, than inexpensive models.

The differences

At first glance professional saxes look just like the more affordable models. To *see* the differences you need to take a close look. To *hear* the differences you need to be a fairly experienced player. Here are some of those differences.

Time and effort

Expensive saxophones cost more because more time and effort are put into their manufacture and better quality materials are used. Making them involves more handwork and craftsmanship, as well as research and development.

The metal

Both sound and price are influenced by the precise composition of the metal and the way in which it is worked and finished. Budget saxes will usually not have the depth of sound that a more expensive one may offer you, or they may not play in tune quite so well.

The parts

Expensive saxophones have expensive parts. Stronger rods, better springs, adjustable keys, or a sterling silver crook, to name a few examples. Such an instrument not only sounds better – it's also likely to be more reliable, last longer and stay in adjustment longer than a budget saxophone. This is one of the reasons that higher quality instruments generally maintain their resale value better than cheap ones.

Getting help

You do need to be a fairly experienced player in order to tell how good a sax is. So if you're a first-time buyer, you may have a problem; you won't be able to tell whether those squeaks are your fault or the instrument's. The solution is easy. Always take along someone who can play, or at least go to a store where a member of the sales staff can demonstrate a number of instruments to you.

Trying it out

What's the most important advice of all? Never buy an instrument without hearing it first. A good music shop will give you all the time you need to try out a number of horns. Check chapter 6, *A Good Sax*, for everything you need to pay attention to when you are doing that. All instruments in a good shop will have been properly adjusted, too. If they haven't been then you can't really judge them properly – because you won't be able to play them properly.

Maintenance

Adjusting a saxophone can only be done properly by a specialist repairer, so it may pay off to buy your instrument in a shop that has its own repair department. If you've bought a new sax, it may need to be adjusted a couple of times during the first few months. Often, although not always, this is included in the price paid for the instrument. If you want to know more about this then go to chapter 10, *Cleaning and Maintenance.*

Rental instruments

Some shops rent out instruments. That'll give you some time to see if the instrument really suits you. Rental prices start at around £18/$25 a month. Many shops also offer rent-to-own programmes.

How expensive is it really?

Professional flute players might spend over £3000/$4000 on their instrument, if they want one handmade of gold or platinum. Pianists and violinists may do the same. Sax players don't, however. Why not? Simply because there are no saxophones that cost that much. The cheapest sax is never particularly cheap, but compared to many other instruments the most expensive ones aren't all that expensive.

OLD VERSUS NEW

Almost every saxophone shop sells used instruments as well as new ones. Are they much cheaper? Not always. For a playable secondhand tenor in mint condition you can easily pay £500/$750 or more – and you could buy a brand new horn for that price.

Overhaul costs

Why are used saxes so expensive? Because they often need a partial or a complete overhaul before they're fit for sale, taking both time and money. On the other hand, buying a modern sax secondhand will still be a bit less expensive than buying the same model new. As a rough guide, expect to pay about 70 percent of the list price for a secondhand instrument.

Vintage horns

Some sought-after vintage horns may even be worth more than new ones, including American instruments from the Fifties and early Sixties or a French Selmer of the same era. Many players – mainly jazz musicians – prefer these instruments because they feel they sound richer, fatter and warmer than new ones. The same words, by the way, are often used to describe the sound of vintage guitars and vintage cymbals, among other instruments.

The good and the bad

Of course, not every old sax is a good instrument. In the 'good old days' they built their share of bad horns too. The first saxophones, if you're talking about really old instruments, were not identical to the ones that were made in later years. Examples of well-known older saxes (good ones, that is) are given in chapter 14, *The Brands*.

The differences: left, an alto from 1864 built by the inventor Adolphe Sax. Right, a modern alto, which is a little larger.

Commercial versus private

Used saxes can be found most easily in music shops, but of course you will also come across them in pawnshops or advertised in the classified sections of newspapers and music journals. It may be cheaper to buy a used instrument from a private individual than at a store, but one of the advantages of buying a used instrument in a shop is that you can go back if something needs to be readjusted, for instance. A music store should also give you a guarantee on your purchase, and a private seller obviously won't. Finally, a good dealer will not charge you more than the instrument's worth, whereas a private seller might, either because they don't know any better, or they think that you don't.

Bring someone along

If you're planning to buy a used sax it's more important than ever to bring along someone who knows saxophones, especially if you're answering a classified ad. If you don't, you might easily pass up an excellent instrument at a bargain price that merely needs a bit of attention. Or far worse, you might get stuck with a useless, unrepairable mess.

Assessment

Another way to avoid paying too much is to take the sax you're considering to a repairer who can assess its value. They can also tell you what repairs may be necessary, and how much they will set you back.

Leaky as a sieve

Any good sax can be brought back into top condition, even if it's so leaky that you can't play it. But it isn't cheap. If you buy a leaky instrument you should be prepared to pay up to £300/$400 to get it into decent playing condition.

AND FINALLY...

You'll probably think that the most beautiful sax sound is the one your favourite sax player produces. So should you buy the same horn? Not necessarily so. Even if you use exactly the same sax, mouthpiece and reed, your sound is bound to be different.

Who's blowing the horn

Ask a horn player to play a couple of different saxes, and you will hear pretty much the same sound both times. Ask two players to play the same sax, and they will sound quite different to one another. The sound is determined by the player, rather than by the instrument.

More than the price

The price of playing saxophone is more than just the price you paid for your horn. The maintenance your horn needs to keep it in the best working order usually costs around £40/$50 a year, depending on usage and the skill of the repairer. Reeds are the only other recurrent expense, at about £15/$25 for a box of ten. If you want to raise the value of your instrument you can buy a better mouthpiece, or a handmade crook. These can be valuable investments, although they only make sense if both you and your horn are worth it.

Catalogues, magazines and the Internet

The more you know, the more likely you are to buy the best saxophone that you can get. Brochures and catalogues of the various brands are a good source of basic information, while reviews and articles on saxophones, mouthpieces and reeds can be found in a variety of magazines. The Internet is handy for up-to-date product information too, with many commercial sites as well as saxophone newsgroups. More about these and other resources can be found on page 113 and following.

Fairs and conventions

One last tip: if a music trade-fair or convention is being held anywhere near you, go and check it out. Besides being able to try out and compare a considerable number of instruments, you will also have the chance to meet plenty of product specialists, as well as numerous fellow horn players who will always provide information and inspiration.

6. A GOOD SAX

The material. The exact dimensions of the tube. The key system. The pads. The intonation. When it comes to finding the differences between one sax and the other, there are a lot of things that need to be looked for or listened to. What makes a sax a good sax? And what makes one sax better than another? This chapter covers everything you need to think about if you want to buy the best horn you can buy.

The outside of a horn is not the most important element – but it's the most visible one, so that's where this chapter starts. If you want to start playing right away without taking a closer look at the instrument and its parts, then skip to chapter 9 (page 72).

Brass

Nearly all saxophones are made from brass, a mixture of copper and zinc. Brass can be finished in a variety of ways, but it is often coated with a glossy lacquer. This is usually transparent or with a light gold tint (*gold lacquer*). Brass with a higher copper content has a distinctive reddish tint.

Silver

Silver-plated saxes, which you'll only find in the higher price ranges, are often said to sound a bit less bright, warmer or more intimate than lacquered instruments. And of course, there are those who will swear that it's the other way around – you'll have to make up your own mind.

(Black) nickel
Nickel-plated saxes, which were widely produced until well into the Sixties, have the same general tint as silver-plated horns but look a bit shinier. Some of the black saxophones that you may come across are not lacquered black, but rather plated with black nickel.

Gold
Gold plating is rare, but there are a limited number of gold-plated crooks around and some brands will be glad to supply you with an instrument that is entirely gold-plated.

Any colour
Besides the black nickel-plated saxes mentioned above there are also lacquered horns in pretty much any colour you can think of.

Variations
The key system is not always finished the same way as the rest of the instrument. It might be nickel-plated while the rest is gold lacquered, or the body may have a matt lacquer while the keys have a high gloss finish or vice versa. Not all brands and series offer these options.

Engraving
Most saxes have a design engraved on the bell. Some brands offer the option of instruments without this decoration.

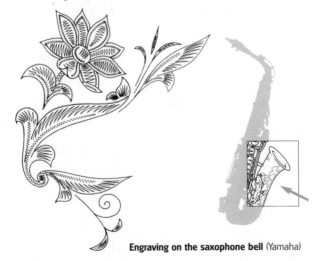

Engraving on the saxophone bell (Yamaha)

A CLOSER LOOK

For the most part, a saxophone's appearance has very little to do with its sound. Taking a closer look may tell you more. Not only about the sound, but also about how long you can expect it to last and other intimate details.

Well made

When inspecting a sax, check how solid it looks and feels and how sturdily it's built. Compare an affordable instrument with a very expensive one, and take note of the differences. How are the key guards attached to the bell and the body? Does the instrument look as if it can survive a knock or two, or does everything feel thin and fragile? Detachable bells and bows, which are found on certain models, are handy when it comes to removing dents in the body.

Tone holes

Run your finger along the edges of the tone holes. The smoother and thicker they are, the less they will eat into the pads and the less chance of leaks developing. To prevent leaks, the tone hole edges should be level as well. Some saxes have tone holes with rolled edges, providing a round and very pad-friendly collar, but very few new instruments offer this feature.

Ordinary tone hole and tone hole with folded collar

Posts

The posts that hold the key system in place can be soldered onto the body either individually or in groups, by means of metal strips. The latter technique is often referred to as *rib* or *ribbed construction*, as opposed to *post construction*. A ribbed construction basically makes for a sturdier instrument. Some say the ribs constrict the sound a bit, but you'll have a hard time trying to hear the difference.

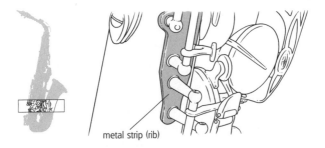

metal strip (rib)

Saxophone with ribbed construction

THE KEY SYSTEM

The key system includes the keys, rods, springs and everything else that moves when you're playing. A lot of progress has been made in this area over the years. The action has become quite a bit smoother, it has been given a more natural feel and adjustable side and palm keys have been introduced, to mention just a few examples.

Nineteen

The very first saxes had nineteen keys. More and more were added, as the illustration on page 27 shows. Other keys disappeared over the years. Modern saxes generally have 24 or 25 keys, the 25th being the high F-sharp (F♯) key which was added in the Sixties and is now pretty much a standard item.

No high F-sharp key

Some saxophonists do not like this key, as they feel it affects the instrument's timbre for the worse. It's possible for an

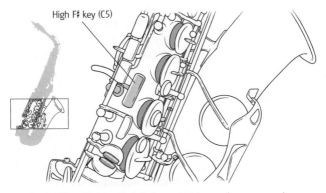

High F♯ key (C5)

The high F♯ key. The tone hole is located higher up (see next page).

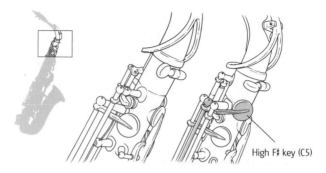

High F♯ key (C5)

Saxes without (left) and with a high F♯ key (right)

experienced player to reach the note without using the extra key.

Even higher

The same goes for high G, a key that is only found on the occasional soprano sax. The highest notes on a sax, played by using special fingerings and air stream adjustments, are known as the *altissimo register* or as the *high harmonics*. On the other end of the spectrum you have the low A that can be found on most modern baritones. In order to reach that low, these horns are slightly longer than B-flat baritones.

Automatic octave key

Sometimes saxes are promoted by highlighting their *automatic octave key*. It sounds impressive, but it has actually been pretty standard since the Thirties. When you press the octave key, the mechanism 'automatically' determines which of the two octave vents is opened. The lower octave vent opens for the notes D to G-sharp, while for A and higher the upper octave vent opens and the first one closes automatically. In the old days saxes had a separate key for each octave vent.

Automatic G-sharp

The *automatic G-sharp* or *articulated G-sharp*, introduced on expensive instruments in the Thirties, is now standard on nearly every sax. It opens the G-sharp key when you are using the low C-sharp, B or B-flat key. As a result your left little finger doesn't need to make a troublesome shift when moving between one of these notes and a G-sharp. The system has one drawback: your little finger has to work harder because it needs to operate several keys simultaneously. If this is a problem, some saxes have the option of disengaging it.

Non-sticking G-sharp
Some effective, yet simple solutions have impressive names. The *G-sharp Pad Cup Lifting Mechanism*, for instance, is no more than a small lever that helps open the G-sharp key, which can have a tendency to stick.

Articulated C-sharp
If you play a low B or low B-flat, your little finger can easily get stuck on the C-sharp key, with the result that a C-sharp sounds instead of whatever it was you intended. Most saxes therefore have a small rod that closes the C-sharp key as soon as the low B or B-flat key is depressed. This *articulated C-sharp* ensures that you get the note you want.

Does it suit you?
Every alto sax is the same size. All tenors are the same size. However, it is likely that one make or series will suit you better than another. Even such a minor detail as the exact location of the eye for the sling hook may make it difficult for you to balance the instrument properly.

Side and palm keys
The exact position of the side and palm keys is equally important. If they sit high and you have small hands you may find them difficult to reach, or you may open them accidentally. Some saxes come with adjustable keys, either

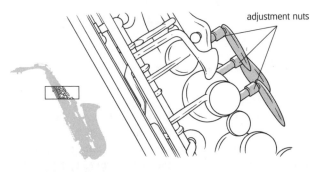

Adjustable palm keys (Keilwerth)

as standard or as an option. Examples are the G-sharp, high F, low C-sharp and palm keys.

Adjusting keys

Alternatively, a saxophone repairer can adjust an instrument to your liking by reshaping keys or by replacing some felts or corks with thinner or thicker ones. Should the side or palm keys be too low, a set of *key risers* can make them more accessible. As an alternative, you can have them built up with cork or epoxy resin.

Sitting down

A sax is best played standing up, as this gives you better control over your breath. Nevertheless it's a good idea to check how a prospective horn feels when sitting down since that's how you'll be expected to play in a wide variety of groups and orchestras.

Spatula keys

The shape of the little keys varies from one brand or series to another. The same goes for the front F, which may either be a pearl key or a spatula key. Finding the instrument that suits you best remains a matter of trial and error.

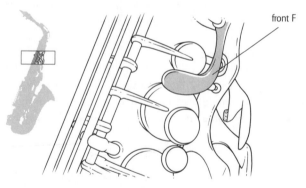

front F

Sax with a spatula key for the front F

Flat or concave

On some saxes the key pearls are flat, while on others they may be slightly concave to allow your fingers to sit on the key more comfortably. There are also manufacturers who use a combination of flat and concave ones to help you know where your fingers are from the feeling.

The thumb hook

A lot of today's thumb hooks allow both height and angle to be adjusted. Some players find plastic thumb hooks feel more comfortable than metal ones. Although metal hooks are said to be sturdier, they can discolour or even irritate your skin. A cheap and effective solution to this problem is to slide a *thumb saver* over it.

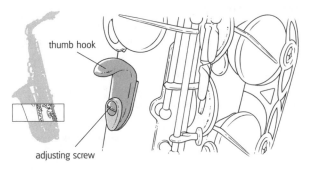

Adjustable thumb hook

THE ACTION

Once you've tried a number of instruments you may notice that one plays more quickly, easily or comfortably than another. The way that the key system feels and plays is called the *action*, and the quality of the action largely depends on the resistance of the many springs that help open and close the keys and pads, as well as on the quality of the general workmanship of the system.

Heavy or light

All the keys should have a similar resistance, giving the instrument what's known as a balanced action. If the keys require a lot of pressure to operate you'll be working too hard. A very light action, on the other hand, keeps the keys from responding quickly and precisely. Adjusting the action to your preference is a job for a repairer.

Play

In order for the pads to seal the tone holes in exactly the same place, time after time, there should not be any play in the rods. Such play slows down the action, too, and causes squeaks and rattles. Similarly, the rollers on the little finger keys are supposed to roll, and not be loose or noisy.

Key height

If a key feels as if it has to be pressed a long way down before anything really happens the key height may be out of adjustment. Besides being awkward in fast passages, this may result in bad intonation (see page 40). Key height can be adjusted pretty easily.

Sticking and bouncing

A key should return to its resting position quickly and smoothly as soon as it's released – it's not supposed to stick, bounce or rattle. You can test this by lightly depressing each and every key cup, quickly sliding your finger off it sideways and seeing what happens. And listening to what happens. Faulty adjustment is one possible cause of clattering keys, and missing felts or corks are another. On older instruments, felts may have become compressed.

PADS

On a classical guitar gut strings have long been replaced by nylon ones and drummers play on plastic heads, calf skin drumheads now being a thing of the past. But saxophones still have leather pads. Why? Because these still work the best, according to most sax players. However, alternative, non-leather pads are beginning to make their way onto the market.

Leather and felt

The most common pads are felt discs covered with a thin

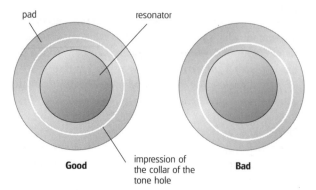

Good   impression of
the collar of the
tone hole   **Bad**

The impression of the collar of the tone hole must be exactly in the middle of the pad

layer of sheep, goat or kid leather. To seal the tone holes properly the pads must be exactly centred over the holes. In order to check this look at the impression that the edge of the tone hole has left on the pad.

Resonators

Resonators, the small plastic or metal discs in the middle of each pad, add clarity to the sound and make the sax more responsive. If your horn seems too bright you might consider using pads without resonators. Another option is to have pads with a layer of brass foil under the skin, providing a flat surface and an extended life span.

Non-leather pads

Leather pads don't last a lifetime, since they are constantly getting wet – from the moisture in your breath – and drying out again. Under these conditions, just like leather shoes, they will not last forever. With non-leather pads made of synthetic materials or rubber compounds you avoid these problems. When these new pads were first introduced they met with quite a lot of resistance, but over the years they have been continually improved, and acceptance has grown accordingly.

More expensive

Synthetic pads are more expensive than leather pads. On the other hand, they require less maintenance, they're more reliable and they last longer. In addition, their reduced weight is said to improve the action.

PLAYING

To be able to find out how good a sax really is you have to play it. If you're a complete beginner, ask an experienced player to perform the tests on the following pages.

The mouthpiece

To test a sax you need a good mouthpiece. The one that comes with the instrument might not be the best one for you, or for the horn itself. If you have your own mouthpiece then that's the one to use, and if you need to know more turn to chapter 7, *Mouthpieces and Crooks*.

The reed
Since the reed is what actually generates the sound, the need for a good one is obvious. Chapter 8 tells you everything you have to know, and remember that everything mentioned in this chapter will be affected to a certain extent by the quality of the reed you're using.

The trickiest ones
The first test on every sax is to play a B, by pressing key 1 with your left index finger. From there you go down the scale, note by note, until you reach low B-flat. The lowest notes are the trickiest ones. If the sax is leaking even a tiny bit, you'll have trouble getting them to speak.

Light pressure
In order to really put the sax to the test, use as little air pressure as possible, and press the keys as lightly as you can. If you need to blow harder or squeeze the keys to get a note out, something is probably wrong.

Pop
Playing the keys without blowing the horn should result in a series of resonant popping sounds – the sound that pads make when they seal the tone holes properly. Unfortunately, hearing a solid, reassuring pop every time you close a key doesn't necessarily mean that you found yourself a fantastic horn.

INTONATION
You use your embouchure and your air stream to determine the exact pitch of a note. This takes some time to learn, but it's something you simply have to do; unfortunately a sax is never perfectly in tune with itself. The better in tune the sax is to begin with, the less you'll need to adjust it in your playing.

Why not?
Why doesn't a sax play exactly in tune with itself? This would only be possible if, for example, each note had its own octave vent, and there's simply no room on the instrument to do that. Another reason? The pitch of a note is largely determined by the position of the tone hole on

the tube. If a tone hole is too high up, that note will be too high. Since the positions of all tone holes are interrelated, it's difficult, if not impossible, to put all the holes exactly where they should be. For instance, high C-sharp is often a bit sharp. If manufacturers were to do something to remedy it they would risk making other notes go flat. It's all a matter of compromise, basically, just as with many other instruments.

Extreme cases
On some extremely poor quality saxophones some of the tone holes may be in the wrong place altogether. Instruments like that are nearly impossible to play in tune. A pointer: if the price of a new horn *seems* too good a bargain to be true, perhaps it *is* too good to be true.

The violin and the double bass
You can spot an out-of-tune high note more easily than an out-of-tune low note. That's why it's better to have a neighbour who's learning to play the double bass than one who's trying to master the violin. The same is true for saxes. It's easier to play a tenor sax in tune than an alto, and an alto is in turn easier to play in tune than a soprano.

Open C-sharp
The first way to test the intonation on a sax is to play the notes from open C-sharp (no keys depressed) to D (all pearl keys depressed, plus the octave key). The C-sharp is usually a bit flat, while the D is usually a fraction sharp.

Other intervals
Another test of tuning is to play larger intervals, such as fifths (C–G, D–A, and so on) and octaves (C, with and without the octave key, and so on) and check whether they sound in tune. Try using an electronic tuner in this process to make doubly sure.

Tuning, leaks and key openings
The intonation of a sax can only be judged if it has been tuned (see chapter 9, *Before and After*). If your sax is tuned to too high or too low a pitch individual notes may also be out of tune with each other. Out-of-tune notes can also be the result of poorly adjusted key heights. Keys that open

too wide may result in sharp notes, and vice versa. A leaky sax will have poor intonation, too. Refer to page 46 for tips on locating leaks.

Advanced testing
Here's a tuning test for advanced players. By adjusting your air stream you can play a range of notes without changing your fingering. You are then playing the *harmonic series* or the *harmonics* of that note. Fingering a low B-flat, the first harmonic is the B-flat an octave higher, the second is the F above that, then the next B-flat and the D follow, and so on. If these notes are all in tune and speak easily, you have found yourself a decent saxophone as far as tuning goes.

Your intonation
So far, the term 'intonation' has been used in relationship to the instrument itself, but it can also refer to the skill of the player. If you have good intonation you can play in tune even on an out-of-tune horn.

Best buy
The worse in tune a sax is the better a player you have to be to make it sound acceptable, so beginners are better off buying a sax that plays in tune easily rather than one with a beautiful sound and poor intonation. The ideal buy, however, is the one that does both well.

BUT DOES IT SOUND GOOD?
The previous pages dealt with checking the technical and mechanical condition of a saxophone and with finding out if it can play in tune. There's one more question, though: how does it sound? Here are a few ideas.

Five players, five sounds
Unleash five different sax players on any one instrument and you'll get five different sounds, since the sound of a sax largely depends on the player. So does it really help to have someone else play a few different horns for you? Yes. As different as they may sound on each horn, the character of the horn remains constant. The one that sounds brighter when your friend plays it will probably sound brighter when you play it, too.

The wall

If you're going to compare a few different saxes yourself, do so standing near a wall and aiming the bell towards it. This makes it easier to judge the sound, as it bounces back to you instead of disappearing into the room.

Different saxes, different sounds

Why does a saxophone sound the way it does? The exact composition and thickness of the brass play a role, as does the way in which the metal has been worked and finished. The smoothness of the inside of the instrument is also a factor. One of the main elements, however, is the actual shape of the tube: how it progresses from narrow to wide (the *bore*). In the end, these technicalities and specifications are less important, less interesting, and less musical than the sound that comes out of the horn.

Sounds and words

When reading or talking about the sounds of saxophones, you may come across words ranging from thin, broad and fat, to solid, bright, green, dull, shallow, adventurous, brown, boring, blue and heavy, and so on. Words that have a different meaning for everyone. The more you talk and read about sounds, however, the easier it gets to picture and describe the sound of your favourite horn. And that may make it easier to find it.

Classical or funk?

Every sax has its own character. You like it a lot or a little, you don't like it all, or you can't make up your mind. This is a matter of taste, as long as you make sure you don't end up with the 'wrong' instrument. Some makes and series, for example, are meant primarily for classical music and although you can still use such a horn to wail away in a funk band another instrument would probably be more suitable.

Things to listen for

When trying out a sax, listen for the quality of tone, its evenness, how easily it speaks, and how well it plays at the extremes of volume.

Evenness

Every horn sounds fuller and fatter in its low register. In

the high register, the tone will be thinner and more compact. With a good instrument, that change will occur gradually. To test this, play the sax from high to low, and from low to high, both loud and soft. If the tone quality suddenly changes from one note to the next or if certain notes seem to jump out you'll be better off trying another horn. A very critical spot is the break between registers, from open C-sharp to the D a semitone above it. This D is the first note to use the octave key when you play an ascending scale.

Response
This test also allows you to hear how the sax responds. Do all the notes come out smoothly and easily even when you're playing softly in the low register? The more smoothly an instrument responds the easier it will be to play in general.

Loud and soft
Play the sax as loud as you can. Does it go completely out of control, or can you produce a focused, tight sound even at a high volume level? Try playing very softly. Do the notes speak just as smoothly, or does the horn need to be played loudly to get a resonant and full-bodied sound?

USED INSTRUMENTS
If you're thinking of purchasing a used instrument there are a few additional things you need to keep an eye and an ear open for. And a nose, too. Special tips on buying vintage instruments from the Sixties or earlier can be found at the end of this chapter.

The lacquer
You don't need a microscope to spot the difference between new and old instruments; the latter often have considerably less lacquer. How much difference does this make? Not a great deal, in fact, as far as the sound is concerned. Although a gorgeous, shiny new instrument can look very tempting and play superbly, you may prefer an older horn for its sound, its feel, or both. Used saxes, especially vintage ones, can be just as good a buy as new ones costing the same amount.

New lacquer

You can also come across older saxes that sport a beautiful coat of lacquer, but in this case the chances are that it has been relacquered. Bear in mind that preparing an instrument for this process requires a lot of polishing, which thins the metal and may lead to play in the key system. If too much lacquer has been applied, the sound will be dull. On the other hand there are saxophones around that sound better after having been relacquered.

Dents

A small dent in the bell is not a catastrophe, but the higher it is on the instrument, the more annoying it becomes. On the crook even a tiny dent can affect both the intonation and the timbre for the worse. Dents in the body can dislocate parts of the key system, preventing certain keys from functioning properly. They can also alter the rigidity of the body, which may influence the tone. The cost of removing dents depends on how severe they are and how hard they are to reach.

Play

If a used sax has a feather-light action there's a chance that the springs are old and tired. If they can't be adjusted (*retensioned*) to be firm enough again, they'll have to be replaced. There may also be too much play in the rods. A rod is supposed to rotate, not wobble back and forth. To inspect an instrument thoroughly you need to check all the moving parts for excess play. Is even a little bit of play something to worry about? Yes, because it will only get worse. A saxophone repairer can help alleviate play, of course, but the worse it is the trickier and more expensive the job will be.

Rust

Check carefully for signs of rust at the ends of rods and on screws. Rusty parts can drastically slow down the mechanism.

Solder

Visible globs of solder are a sign that the instrument has been sloppily repaired. A neat job is preferable, but a sloppy repair isn't necessarily an ineffective repair. However, it's a good idea to be particularly careful when inspecting such an instrument.

The crook
You may come across a used saxophone with a crook that wasn't made for it. This could mean trouble, in terms of intonation. If you want to know more, see page 61.

A snug fit
Always check the *crook cork* that the mouthpiece fits onto. Is it in good condition, not falling apart, badly worn or overly compressed, and does it fit your mouthpiece properly? Check to see that the crook fits snugly into the body and that there's no play in the joint. If there is, air will escape, affecting both the intonation and the response of the horn.

Crooked crook
And then there's the tenor which sounded as though its D, E and F keys didn't seal properly; yet all the pads did what they were supposed to do. The problem was in the crook, which was bent down ever so slightly, as though someone had been leaning on it. As tenors have vulnerable crooks, you should check it by running your fingers along its sides. The crook should be perfectly round throughout its length.

The pearls
Has the mother-of-pearl worn off the keys? Then you can be sure the sax has seen quite a bit of use. Still, there's no need to worry; saxes don't wear out in the way that cars do, and the pearls can be replaced quite simply.

Leaking pads?
Do you suspect that a pad is leaking? Slide a piece of paper under it, close the key gently and pull the paper away. If you don't feel any resistance, you've probably found your leak.

Leak light
However, if the low C, for example, doesn't sound properly, it doesn't necessarily follow that the C key is the culprit. There might be a leak higher up the instrument. Since this

may be hard to determine while playing, repairers use a so-called *leak light* which they insert into the instrument. In this way you can see where the leak is by the light that escapes.

A truly bad horn?

Even if the instrument is leaky all over, don't immediately assume it's an absolute disaster. It does mean, however, that it needs a lot of work. Some saxes can be cured with just a few new pads, others may need a complete overhaul, which may set you back at least £160/$200, and possibly three times as much (see page 26).

Clatter test

Always check used saxophones for clattering keys. One key at a time, listen carefully for metal on metal noise and rattles which indicate worn or missing felts or corks, bent rods, bent keys or other problems. Some problems are simple to repair, others aren't. Buying a sax at a reputable music store can prevent expensive surprises.

Too high, too low

Some older instruments have a higher or lower standard tuning, and it may be hard or impossible to tune them to the other instruments in a group. Will you have any problems using such a horn for solo practising? Yes, actually; you will end up getting used to its specific pitch. When changing to a horn with standard tuning you'll have to adjust both your intonation and your hearing.

HP, LP

Saxes with a higher standard tuning can be identified by the abbreviation HP (high pitch) or by the indication A=902 or A=451, the standard tuning being 440*. The letters LP or a number below 440 or 880 indicates an instrument in low pitch. These indications are usually located below the thumb hook, or on the bell. You can also tell the pitch by the length of the horn: a higher-pitched instrument will be an inch or so shorter than a sax with standard tuning, and a lower-pitched one an inch or so longer.

---

* *Instruments are commonly tuned to concert A, usually 440 or 442 vibrations per second (440 or 442 Hertz) for the A above middle C.*

Phew

If you are looking at an older used sax and a terrible smell comes wafting out of the case when it's opened, you are looking at a poorly-maintained instrument, an instrument that hasn't been played for a long, long time, or simply at a smelly case. Don't worry: the instrument can be cleaned, and cases are easily replaced.

VINTAGE SAXOPHONES

Many professional jazz and fusion players prefer older instruments, which are often said to sound darker and fatter than today's horns and to offer bigger dynamic range. If you do too, you may have to put up with certain things. One player put it this way: 'If I fall in love with the sound of a sax, there's usually something or other wrong with the instrument. It's really out of tune in one spot, for instance. Okay, well then... so be it.'

Not all the same

Not every vintage sax is a good one. Moreover, in the old days, when horns were still made by hand, the differences between individual saxes were greater than they are today. One well-known vintage horn, therefore, may not be as good as the other, even if it's the same make and series of the same year. So watch out. For examples of well-known older saxes refer to chapter 14, *The Brands*.

Control

Vintage saxes are more versatile than new ones. There's more to fool around with: the tone, the way it sounds, the way it feels. On the other hand, you have to be able to really exert a lot of control in order to harness that flexibility and to play in tune; vintage instruments are known for their intonation problems, and they require better air stream control.

Heavier action

The action is often heavier than on most modern saxes. It may take your fingers a while to get used to it, especially on tenors and baritones. Altos are less of a problem as the keys are slightly closer together, and you're moving less of a weight of metal.

Position and shape of keys

In the old days manufacturers knew (or cared) less about the optimal positioning and shape of the keys. New saxes lie under the hands better and play more comfortably, just as a new car drives more easily than one from the Thirties. As just one example, today's octave key, shaped as a sort of crescent around the thumb rest, is a lot easier to play than the old-fashioned button key.

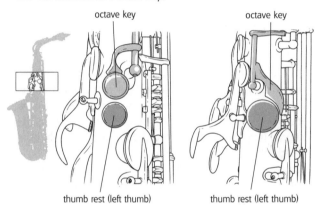

Left: Round octave key on a Buescher Truetone, 1927
Right: A modern octave key. The palm keys are also different.

Some have them, some don't

Older saxes may have keys that newer ones lack. An example is the G-sharp trill key, operated by the right middle finger to trill between G and G-sharp. It was used on certain German and American saxes made before 1940, just like the special key to trill between D and D-sharp.

Old mouthpieces

If you find yourself a horn from before the Forties, it may be difficult to find a suitable mouthpiece. Modern mouthpieces usually don't work well with these instruments. A couple (or a lot) of notes may not respond well, and the entire sax can sound out of balance or out of tune.

Many years

Apart from their sound and their romantic image, vintage saxes have one more advantage: if you maintain and play them properly they will retain their value for many years to come, and it may even increase.

7. MOUTHPIECES AND CROOKS

Give a poor player a top-notch instrument, and they won't sound that much better. Give a top-notch player an inferior horn, and they won't sound that much worse. It's the player that has the strongest influence on the sound. Next come the reed and the mouthpiece, both of which play a substantial role.

Reeds are discussed fully in chapter 8, but first, here's everything you need to know about mouthpieces, crooks and ligatures.

The best mouthpiece is the one that allows you to do everything you want to most easily. Just like a pair of shoes, a mouthpiece has to fit. In this case, what fits is determined by your technique, your embouchure, the shape of your mouth and the position of your teeth – and the sound you're looking for. All of this largely outweighs any of the technical jargon you may come across in your pursuit of the perfect mouthpiece. Still, it doesn't hurt to shed some light on these technical terms.

How it works

The vibration of the reed causes the air inside the mouthpiece to vibrate in its turn. Exactly how that air vibrates has a lot to do with the sound that results, and the design of the mouthpiece (material, shape and dimensions) plays a crucial role in this process.

Your voice sounds different in a bathroom to the way it does in an average living room. A mouthpiece has a 'room' too: the *chamber*. Different chambers produce different sounds.

What's what

- The *tone chamber* has a *window*, which is covered by the reed. The edges of the window are called the *rails*.
- The *table* is the flat part where the reed is fixed to the mouthpiece.
- The distance between the tip of the reed and the tip of the mouthpiece is the *tip opening*.
- The area where the mouthpiece curves away from the reed is the *facing* or the *lay*.
- The *baffle* is a raised section inside the mouthpiece chamber. A pronounced baffle is also called a *wedge*.

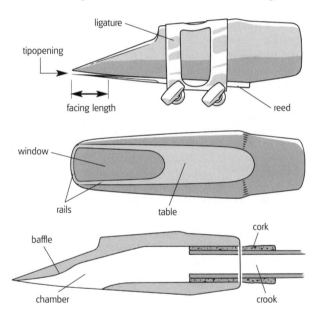

A mouthpiece: side view, bottom view and cross-section

What counts

The tip opening, the length of the facing, the shape of the baffle and the size of the chamber are the most important variables affecting the sound and playability of a mouthpiece.

Open or closed

Sax players talk about *open* or *closed mouthpieces*. An open mouthpiece is one with a large tip opening. This provides a bigger sound but requires a good embouchure and well-developed breath control. A closed mouthpiece, with a small tip opening, plays more easily, and creates a less 'open', more easily controlled type of sound.

Beginners

Most budget saxophones come with a medium-close mouthpiece, which is a good choice for a beginner. The quality of these mouthpieces may not be what you're looking for, however. Some good alternatives, recommended for beginners, are the Selmer C*, the Yamaha 5C and the Vandoren A25. These and similar mouthpieces make playing relatively painless and help you learn to pitch the notes accurately.

Hundreds to choose from

Once you've been playing for a while you can enhance your sound with a professional mouthpiece – and there are literally hundreds to choose from. There's only one way to find out which one suits you best: try them. All of them? No, not really. Here are a few pointers.

A handful will do

Depending on how well you play, what you play, and what you feel you need you can easily make a basic selection of a handful of mouthpieces, or have a member of the sales staff make a selection. Then you can get down to business, trying them out one by one. How comfortable do they feel, what do they sound like, how responsive are they and how easily do they play? Use your own sax, of course, as a mouthpiece is more than likely to behave differently on another instrument. If you can't find what you're looking for, then try a different selection.

Triage

You may find it hard to choose what you like best even from a relatively small selection. A good way to handle things is to start with three mouthpieces, replace the one you like least, try them again, replace the one you like least. And carry on.

Blending in

There are special mouthpieces for classical music, with a darker, tighter, prettier, rounder type of sound – a sound that blends well with other instruments. These mouthpieces suit concert and marching bands, too. At the other end of the spectrum, you'll come across mouthpieces that produce a lot of volume, and a bright sound with a raw, sharp edge to it. They're not meant to blend at all, but to make your sound stand out, even in a loud band.

Somewhere in between

In between these extremes there are mouthpieces that have been designed with a jazz combo in mind, or a big band. The more you know about mouthpieces, the more easily you can skip the ones that don't work for you, allowing you to concentrate on the ones that suit your needs. Talk to anyone you can find who knows about the subject. It'll pay off.

The price tag

The price can be a deciding factor in your choice. A good mouthpiece may set you back £60–120/$50–300, but it's possible to pay over £400/$600 for a handmade one, designed to your own specifications and involving many consultations with the maker.

DIFFERENCES

What are the differences between large and small tip openings, or between various facing lengths and baffles? And what is the difference between hard rubber and metal mouthpieces? If you don't care to go into this, you can skip to the buying tips on page 59.

A wide choice

Every manufacturer has their own ideas about the ideal mouthpiece, and you can become very confused wading through the results. With some brands, the facing length increases proportionately with the tip opening. Other makers offer two or three facing lengths, combined with more than ten different tip openings. Others make three mouthpieces with the same facing length and tip opening, each model having its own chamber size or shape.

Corresponding types

Manufacturers have their own individual systems, and they all name and number their mouthpieces accordingly. For example: most brands have an alto mouthpiece with a tip opening of 70/1000" (1.8mm). Brilhart calls it a 3, Dukoff calls it a 5 and Lawton a 6, Vandoren an A15 and Selmer a C**. It's confusing, but the Berg Larsen system seems to make the most sense, since their '70' directly corresponds with the actual size of 70/1000". Fortunately, there are charts available that show the corresponding types and sizes of various brands. You'll find them in music shops and on the Internet.

One consistent feature

There is, at least, one consistent feature in the classification of mouthpieces: the higher the number, the more open the mouthpiece. So a 6 is always more open than a 5 of the same brand. But be aware that it may also be more open than a 7 of another brand.

Stars

To indicate mouthpieces that are in between say, a 5 and a 6, most manufacturers use an asterisk (*). A 5*, pronounced as 'five star', always plays a bit more heavily than a 5. With one brand this is the result of a larger tip opening, whereas another brand uses both a larger tip opening and a longer facing. And a third manufacturer may use a shorter facing – which, with the same tip opening, has the same general effect of making the mouthpiece play more heavily. Yes, it's confusing, but in general the * means an increase of the tip opening by 5/1000".

The entire mouthpiece

When you're buying a mouthpiece, don't concentrate on the tip opening alone. After all, two mouthpieces with the same tip opening can play very differently. One of them may have a larger chamber, another a different facing length or a higher baffle. So always consider the entire mouthpiece, rather than its isolated specifications. And above all, play it.

Everything's interrelated

With mouthpieces, you can't simply line up the variables alongside one another and compare them. After all, two mouthpieces with identical tip openings may be radically different in their respective chambers, facings, baffles, and so on. With that in mind, consider the following tips as a general guide.

TIP OPENING

For any one type of sax, the largest tip opening is generally twice as big as the smallest. The following chart shows some of the main figures.

Most makers give their measurements in thousandths of an inch, so the figure 70, for instance, stands for 70/1000", or .070. If you're more familiar with the metric system, multiply by 0.0254 (0.0254 x 70 = 1.8mm).

	most commonly used	smallest	largest
alto	70–100 (1.8–2.5mm)	50 (1.3mm)	125 (3.2mm)
tenor	90–120 (2–3mm)	55 (1.4mm)	145 (3.7mm)

A mouthpiece with a smaller tip opening:
• produces a smaller, thinner, tighter sound,
• is easier to control,
• makes the instrument respond faster and speak easier,
• is more suitable for classical music and for concert and marching bands,
• produces less volume and is easier to play softly,
• generally requires a harder reed.

A mouthpiece with a larger tip opening:
• produces a larger, more open and more muscular sound, with more body,
• is harder to play,
• is more suitable for jazz, rock and pop, and less for classical music or concert and marching bands,
• produces more volume and is harder to play softly,
• offers more possibilities for controlling the sound and the intonation,
• generally requires a thinner reed.

For beginners
The combination of a very small tip opening and a hard reed is difficult for a beginner, and combining a thin reed and a large tip opening may result in an unsteady sound. Your best bet is a mouthpiece with a small to medium tip opening.

The hardest combination
A large tip opening with a hard reed is one of the hardest

combinations to play. It also produces the biggest sound, which is why you mainly find it on the horns of pro players in jazz, rock and similar styles.

THE FACING LENGTH

A wide tip opening means the reed has to travel over a greater distance, implying that a larger part of the reed has to be able to vibrate. A longer facing allows it that freedom.

A length for each opening

Mouthpieces are usually classified by their tip opening, and most manufacturers have a certain facing length for each tip opening they offer. In other words: the facing length is often dictated by the tip opening.

Choosing a facing length

Some makers, such as Brilhart, Berg Larsen and Meyer, offer mouthpieces with a choice of facing lengths for each tip opening. Each Meyer mouthpiece, for example, is available with a short, medium or long facing. Brilhart is one of the brands where an asterisk refers to the facing length, rather than to the tip opening: a 5 mouthpiece for alto has a facing length of .0875 (22.2mm), while the facing length of the 5* is .0750 (20.6mm).

A longer lay

Many players feel that a longer lay or facing adds greater depth to the sound, and that it makes a large tip opening easier to control. Too long a facing on a mouthpiece with a small tip opening can render the sound dull and lifeless.

The measurements

Alto sax mouthpieces have facing lengths of between approximately .600 (15mm; very short) and .1000 (25mm; very long). On tenor mouthpieces the facings usually lie between .670 (17mm) and 1.175 (30mm).

CHAMBERS, BAFFLES, AND RAILS

As well as the tip openings and facing lengths, the size and shape of the chamber, the baffle and the rails can vary.

The chamber

A number of brands offer a choice of several chamber sizes – another important variable. A larger chamber generally gives a 'larger' darker, rounder or mellower sound. It's also a potentially more versatile mouthpiece, and allows you more control over your sound. With a smaller chamber you get a smaller, tighter, edgier or brighter type of sound.

The baffle

Just as pinching the end of a garden hose gives a more forceful stream of water, a mouthpiece with a baffle produces a more forceful, more aggressive, brighter sound. The higher the baffle, the more your air stream will be condensed and the more powerful its effect will be. A mouthpiece with little or no baffle produces a smoother, warmer, more controllable and more direct sound.

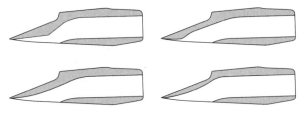

Various baffles (Vandoren)

Brainiac or Headbanger?

Classical orchestras and concert and marching bands require a warm, even sound, so mouthpieces with little or no baffle are the most appropriate. If you prefer heavy and hard, though, you'd better go for a substantial baffle. But you do have to be able to handle it. If you can't, you may end up squeaking in a way that doesn't quite fit the image.

The rails

An advanced player will get a clear, crisp sound out of a mouthpiece with narrow tip and side rails, although for less experienced players this increases the risk of squeaking. Thicker rails give a less brilliant, darker, 'fatter' sound, as well as making playing softly a little easier. Cheap mouthpieces generally have thicker rails – not so much for their tonal or playing characteristics, but because it's easier to make them like that.

A look through the barrel

If you look through the *barrel* of a mouthpiece, at the opposite end from the tip, you'll see a round opening, a square one, or something else altogether. The shape of this opening (the *throat*) has an important effect, too. Generally speaking, an open throat contributes to a dark, fat sound. A constricted throat helps to produce a shallow, bright sound, although it may make you play a little sharp in the upper register.

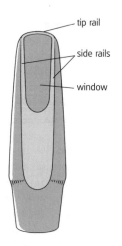

tip rail

side rails

window

MATERIALS

Most mouthpieces are made of either hard rubber or metal. Hard rubber, also known as *ebonite*, is the most common material for classical mouthpieces. Metal mouthpieces are more useful for playing louder. However, there are also edgy sounding hard rubber mouthpieces, just as there are metal mouthpieces for classical players to use.

Comparing dimensions

If you try a hard rubber and a metal mouthpiece with exactly the same dimensions, their sound will be more similar than, say, that of two hard rubber (or two metal) mouthpieces with different dimensions. In the end, the material is less of a critical factor than the dimensions.

Steel or bronze?

It follows that that you can't simply say that bronze mouthpieces sound broader or darker than mouthpieces made of steel, for instance. Again, the result has got more to do with the dimensions than with the material.

Plastic

The least expensive mouthpieces are made of plastic. Their timbre is generally somewhere between that of ebonite and metal mouthpieces. The anonymous plastic mouthpieces which you may come across on low-budget saxes won't normally do too much to enhance your playing.

Other materials

Some manufacturers use other materials, such as a mixture of graphite and other materials, and a limited number even make wooden or crystal mouthpieces.

Size difference

There is one more difference you can easily feel: most metal mouthpieces are slightly smaller than hard rubber ones. Your mouth is therefore slightly less open, which not only feels different but may also result in a slightly more assertive sound.

Bite plate

Because you play with your upper teeth against the mouthpiece, you will immediately feel one of the differences between metal and hard rubber mouthpieces: metal vibrates more strongly. Most metal mouthpieces have a hard rubber *bite plate* that reduces this effect to some extent.

Cushions

If the vibration is still too much, then try using a *mouthpiece cushion.* Some saxophonists use these soft, self-adhesive patches on hard rubber mouthpieces too, preventing teeth marks at the same time. Mouthpiece cushions come in a variety of thicknesses, and if you prefer, you can use two at a time.

BUYING TIPS

Here are a few tips for when you're buying.

- Always keep your embouchure and level of development in mind, when buying a mouthpiece, and try to avoid buying one you can't handle yet. Leave other players, including your idol and your teacher, to their own preferences.
- Mouthpieces are like shoes: the ones that fit your friend may give you blisters, either because of the shape of your feet or the way you walk.
- The rails and table of the mouthpiece should be perfectly smooth. That doesn't necessarily hold for the inside of the mouthpiece, however. Some professional mouthpieces feature a pretty rough looking inside, allowing them to produce the rough sound they were made for.

- The side rails must be of even thickness.
- The tip rail should have the same shape as the tip of the reed.
- If the curvature is not exactly the same on the right and left rails, a mouthpiece is said to have a crooked facing. This is one of the problems you may find in cheap plastic mouthpieces.
- Some mouthpieces cause a sax to play certain notes out of tune. The only way to find out is to retune your sax for each mouthpiece you try out. The tuning line you can draw on the crook cork (see chapter 9) won't work for each different mouthpiece since they vary both in length and in internal dimensions.
- A new mouthpiece may require different reeds from the ones you were using. They may be harder, softer, or even of a different brand.
- And finally: if your sax doesn't play well, have the instrument checked before trying to solve the problem by buying a new mouthpiece. Above all, make sure the problem is not your reed.

A few brands

There are dozens of mouthpiece brands: Berg Larsen, Dukoff, Guardala, Lakey, Otto Link, Meyer, Phil Barone, Ponzol, Rousseau, Rovner and Runyon are just some of the better known examples. Companies such as Brancher, Selmer and Vandoren make both mouthpieces and reeds. Some of the mouthpiece makers aim mostly or solely at the louder end of the market, with mouthpieces made out of hard rubber or metal. Others earned their fame in the classical world, and still others offer mouthpieces for every style of music – just as some offer mouthpieces in all price ranges and others specialize in the professional market.

Is one enough?

Some players buy one good mouthpiece and play it for the rest of their lives. Others never stop trying and buying new models, brands and types. In addition, there are players who use different mouthpieces for different halls, groups or styles of music, and others who play all kinds of music on one and the same mouthpiece. Of course, both groups are convinced that they are the only ones on the one true path.

Used mouthpieces

Since mouthpieces can cost more than £400/$600 and some saxophonists are continually on the lookout for new ones, it follows that there is a lively market for used mouthpieces. Inspect a used mouthpiece carefully for dents and other damage. The tip and rails must be perfectly smooth. Before you play a used mouthpiece, clean it. On page 85 you'll find out how.

THE CROOK

A bad crook can do a bad turn to even the best saxophone. What makes a bad crook? Well, a bad crook is one that makes your sax sound dull or out of tune, or that makes it difficult to get one or more notes to speak. In other words, it's a crook that happens to fit the sax physically, but wasn't made for it. A crook with a dent is a bad one, too. And of course you will find acceptable crooks, good ones and great ones.

A better crook

Most new saxes come with a crook that works perfectly well. Still, most saxes can be improved by buying a better one, just as you can improve the overall picture with a better mouthpiece. A new crook in a price range of £60–120/$100–200 can audibly improve a mediocre sax, giving it a slightly broader and richer sound, and improving its intonation and response. If you have problems getting the low notes to speak then a good crook may help you.

Even better

And you can do even better. Just imagine a handmade, solid sterling silver crook costing about £500/$1000. Such a crook will definitely do great things to your sound – if your sound and your sax are at that level.

The wrong crook

A crook has to fit the saxophone in more than one way. It certainly should not fall off regardless or be impossible to force on to the instrument, but the exact dimensions should match. If not, then the crook octave vent may be in the wrong place relative to the dimensions of the rest of the horn, for example. The result will be intonation problems.

Soprano sax crooks

Quite a few soprano saxes come with both a straight crook and a curved one. Some players feel that the curved variety produces a darker or fuller sound, others take the opposite view – as musicians always do. Perhaps the most important consideration is that a soprano with a curved crook (which looks rather like a baby alto) is a bit less tiring to play, as it needs less physical support. There's a third variation, too; the semi-curved soprano, which basically is a straight instrument with a bell that faces forward.

A new crook

If you're buying another crook, remember that it may require a different mouthpiece. The two are as closely interrelated as mouthpieces and reeds.

LIGATURES

Most standard *ligatures* are straightforward strips of metal, clamped together with one or two screws. In addition to expensive mouthpieces and expensive crooks, there are expensive ligatures as well, costing up to £30/$50 and more. Special ligatures come in a wide variety of designs and materials, from leather to metal mesh.

A 'soft' ligature (BG)

Many choices

Good ligatures enhance the reed's freedom to vibrate, resulting in a better sound and a faster response. Several companies make special ligatures designed to produce a slightly softer, or a much louder sound. There are many different models designed to fit all the different situations a saxophone might be played in.

A metal ligature (BG)

A neat fit

Whichever ligature you choose, make sure it fits your mouthpiece. With a poorly fitting ligature the reed may slip out of place, or not seal to the mouthpiece correctly.

8. REEDS

When you talk or sing your vocal chords vibrate, generating the sound of your voice. When you play the sax, the reed vibrates, generating the sound of your sax. But what are the differences? You can buy reeds in a variety of strengths and types. Reeds can be adjusted. Reeds don't last a lifetime. And, fortunately, reeds are replaceable.

Seven thousandths of an inch (0.02mm) or even less: that's about the thickness of a saxophone reed at the tip. Every note you play, from fierce accents to warm, low whispers, is produced by that thin, vibrating piece of cane.

Tubes and pith

Each reed, if seen under a magnifying glass, consists of innumerable hollow tubes or fibres bundled together with a softer substance in between: the *pith* or *pulp*. The longer you play on a reed, the softer the pith becomes, and the less resilient the fibres get, until it no longer does what it's

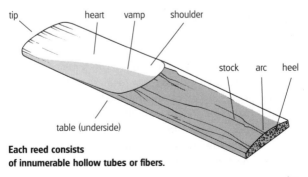

**Each reed consists
of innumerable hollow tubes or fibers.**

supposed to do. If you take good care of a reed it may last two months or more, but it will eventually give up the ghost.

Strength is in numbers

There are soft reeds and hard reeds, classified by number. Most brands go from 1 up to 5, in half steps. A number 2 reed is no thinner than a 4 of the same brand and series, but simply made from a softer piece of cane. Softer reeds have a shorter life. The harder ones allow for a louder, heavier and fuller sound, but they require good breath control and a well-developed embouchure. Softer reeds speak more easily, and you can play very quietly on them. On the other hand they give a slightly thinner, buzzier sound, and intonation may be more difficult. Most beginners find it useful to start with a softer reed, but most players end up graduating to a harder one.

Numbers are relative

Just as with mouthpieces, there are charts which help you compare the different brands. For instance, a 2½ reed of one brand can easily be harder than a 3 reed of another, and you will find similar variations between the various series of one and the same brand. Finally, cane being a natural product, two 'identical' reeds will always differ very slightly.

Your mouthpiece

A mouthpiece with a smaller tip opening requires a harder reed. If the reed is too soft, it will close up and not respond at all. Conversely, a mouthpiece with a large tip opening will play more easily with a softer reed. A good choice for beginners is usually a medium soft reed, such as a 2 or a 2½, on a mouthpiece with a medium small tip opening.

French and American cuts

You're bound to come across the terms *French cut* and *American cut*. French cut reeds, which are mainly used by classical players, have a thinner tip and they're a bit thicker in the heart area. Reeds with an American cut have a slightly thicker tip and less heart, producing a weightier, more focused sound. However, there is no definite standard for these either. If you take a close look at American cut reeds from a variety of brands you'll find at least as many differences as similarities.

French file cut

To make things even more confusing, there's also the *French file cut*. A French file cut is something quite different, as the figure illustrates. Fortunately all brands use the same term to describe the same thing. In the case of reeds with a French file cut a bit of the bark behind the moon-shaped curve of the beginning of the vamp cut has been 'filed' or sanded away. These reeds play more responsively and give a brighter and more open sound. This allows you

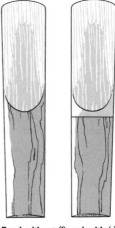

Reed without (l) and with (r) French file cut

to compensate for the effect of an overly mellow, dark sounding mouthpiece.

Tips

- If you're still looking for the perfect reed, buy a variety of individual ones of various brands and strengths, and try them all, bearing in mind that no two reeds are exactly alike, even the ones that come from the same box.
- What should be the main consideration when choosing a certain type of reed? It's supposed to allow you to play what you want to play, as easily as possible.

EXAMINING REEDS

You'll find good, average and poor reeds in almost every box. Careful examination can often weed out the bad ones pretty easily. Asymmetrical reeds, for instance, are not going to help you play your best.

The V

Holding a reed up to the light shows you the profile of the reed cut. The reed should be heavier in the middle, especially in the heart area, and gradually get lighter towards

| V-shape good; a promising reed | An off-centre reed; chance of squeaking | Uneven grain; don't buy | Reed with knots |

the edges and the tip. The upside down V that you will probably see should be symmetrical. An uneven reed may squeak and is unlikely to play well.

Flexibility

By carefully sliding your thumb and index finger along the sides of the reed, you can tell whether the flexibility of the reed is the same on both sides as it should be.

The colour

Greenish-yellow looking reeds cut from very young cane don't generally respond well. If they do, they won't last long. Don't reject the young ones right away, but leave them on one side for a year or so and then try them again. The colour of a good reed varies between gold-yellow and gold-brown.

Grain and knots

The grain should be even throughout the reed, with the fibres densely packed, running evenly and parallel to one another. A reed with knots on the vamp may vibrate unevenly, resulting in an uneven sound.

PLAY-TESTING REEDS

Sax players often buy their reeds by the box, not in order to have a year's supply on hand, but because not every one of those five or ten reeds is going to be good. Reeds are like fruit: one apple tastes better than the other, even though they come from the same tree.

Wet

To get familiar with the reeds you've just bought you'll have to play on them. Wet them first, since a dry reed won't vibrate properly, and if it absorbs moisture while you're playing it is liable to warp. Neither of these things will help give a good sound. The best way to wet a reed is to soak it in a small glass of lukewarm water for no longer than a few minutes. Put it in carefully, tip first.

Glass

You can also lay the reed on a wet piece of glass or mirror. Some reed cases have a special bottom for this purpose. The glass seems to help keep the reed flat, removing waves or wrinkles at the tip. Don't use Plexiglas as it's difficult to keep clean.

Saliva

Most players, however, simply suck on the reed for a while, which works perfectly well. However, since a reed absorbs water more quickly than saliva, and saliva will shorten its life span, it's better to use water. One of the reasons why all reeds wear out in the end is that they are used, after all, in your mouth.

Good and bad reeds

With experience, you'll learn the difference between good and bad reeds. A reed that plays well from the word go may not last long, as the cane may be too young and too soft. At the other extreme, you will also come across reeds that only sound good after a period of breaking in.

Mark your reeds

Here's another tip: test all your new reeds and grade each one, for example by using ++ for the best and −− for the worst ones, with three gradations in between. Set the best reeds aside for performance, and throw the really bad ones away, or leave them aside for a few months, as they may improve with age. And the ones in the middle? Perhaps there's hope even for them. Read on.

Dull or squeaky reeds

Some reeds squeak like crazy, some sound terribly dull. Some are too hard, too soft or of uneven thickness. Or maybe they're not smooth enough, either on the upper side or on the bottom. In short, there are all kinds of unplayable reeds. There are two things you can do with them: either throw them away, or try to adjust them.

ADJUSTING REEDS

Rejecting reeds is quick and easy, but expensive. Learning to adjust reeds takes time and patience – and you use up a lot of reeds doing it. There's no cut-and-dried way to do it; each saxophonist seems to have their own method. Here are some of the basics.

Smoothness is crucial

The facing of the reed must be perfectly smooth in order to seal against the mouthpiece. If it isn't, polish the reed by drawing it over a piece of regular paper a few times. If that doesn't do the trick, use some very fine sandpaper or a *whetstone* (also known as *carborundum stone*), available at hardware stores.

Even motions

Move lengthways along the grain of the reed with smooth, even motions, or carefully sand it in a circular motion. Please, please do avoid sanding the tip. Using sandpaper only works well if it's on a perfectly flat surface. As an alternative, draw a reed knife along the back of the reed. Don't cut, just scrape. An ordinary penknife may do if it's sharp enough.

Too soft

If a reed is too light, you can carefully clip a bit of the tip with a special *reed trimmer* or *reed clipper*, available at music stores. Wet the reed thoroughly before clipping, and never take off more than about 0.04" to 0.06" (1–1½mm). Use a fine nail file or some ultrafine sandpaper to smooth off the edges, always working towards the middle of the tip.

Too hard

A reed that's too thick won't vibrate properly. You can thin the cane out a bit with a piece of *Dutch rush* or *reed rush* (it grows in swamps, but music stores sell it, too). Begin in area 1, as indicated on the following page. Be careful, because the reed is already very thin at this point. If there's no improvement then move on to area 2, then try areas 3 and 4. Always scrape both sides of the vamp evenly to maintain the balance of the reed.

Too shrill

A shrill reed can be scraped in areas 3 and 4. This is not an easy problem to correct.

Too dull

If a reed is too dull, start in area 1, then try areas 3 and 4, and if all else fails, move on to area 2.

Squeaks

Reeds prone to squeaking are often uneven on the sides. You can try to balance such a reed by thinning the thicker side. This is not an easy job, as you can imagine. Test your progress frequently: first play the reed trying to make the right side only vibrate, then switch to the left side. If the sounds differ there's more adjustment needed.

Keep experimenting

Of course there are many other ways to adjust reeds, and there are many tools you can use, varying from ordinary razor blades to burring knives and scrapers. The best way to get the knack of it is to keep experimenting, using old reeds or reeds that you would otherwise throw away.

Keep in mind

- There is one place on a reed that you should avoid, basically: the heart or backbone of the reed, marked on the illustration with an X.
- Good results can never be guaranteed. Even after a couple of hours of hard work you still may be stuck with an unplayable stick.
- What's been taken away is gone forever, so work slowly.
- How much is too much? Think of adjusting reeds as working in hundredths of an inch or tenths of a millimetre.
- When adjusting a reed, test your progress often.

- A mediocre reed can almost always be improved. If you're well practised, so can a bad one. Ruining a great reed doesn't take any experience at all.
- Lots of reed problems? Try another brand, another series or another strength.
- Dull sounding reeds can mellow bright or raucous sounding mouthpieces, and vice versa.
- Don't let a wavy tip bother you too much. The waves will disappear when you play it for a while or, even better, if you wet it (see page 67).
- There are books that shed more light on this subject, *The Art of Saxophone Playing* (see page 113) being just one of them.

Long life

Reeds last as long as they can if you follow these suggestions:

- Always wet your reeds before playing and gently dry them off afterwards, wiping in the direction of the tip (see also page 76).
- Lay a new reed on a flat surface and rub it with the back of a teaspoon, moving toward the tip. This compacts the fibres while making the reed sound a bit brighter.
- Never stand a mouthpiece on end, with or without a reed on it.
- Some players soak their reeds overnight in a 3 percent hydrogen peroxide solution (available at chemists) once in a while, to clean the cane and briefly breath new life into it. Rinse them well with water before playing them again!
- Store your reeds in a proper reed guard (see page 77).

Synthetic reeds

Synthetic reeds made by companies such as BARI and Fibracell last much longer, and they're more consistent than cane reeds. They're louder and more powerful, too, producing a sound that can be described as jagged, fierce, or robust. This type of reed is not an ideal choice for beginners as it's quite resistant and it can present intonation problems.

In between

Rico makes Plasticover reeds: cane reeds that are coated with a thin layer of plastic. They last longer and have a brighter, more powerful sound than plain cane reeds. They also resist moisture and climate changes better.

Some brands

Reeds made by the American companies La Voz and Rico are generally used for jazz, fusion, rock and pop. The French brands Brancher, MARCA and Selmer are more often found on the mouthpieces of classical saxophonists. Vandoren, another French brand, produces reeds for various styles of music. Jazz musicians often use Hemke reeds, which were originally designed for the classical saxophonist.

9. BEFORE AND AFTER

Before you start to play, you have to wet your reed, fix it to the mouthpiece, fit mouthpiece, crook and body together, and tune up. Once you're done, you need to dry the reed and the instrument, and pack up. Sounds like a lot, but it'll be part of your routine before you know it.

The very beginning: the safest way to remove your sax from its case is to grasp it by the bell with one hand, supporting it with the other. If you grab it by the key system, you risk bending things.

Putting on the reed

Wet your reed (see page 67) before putting it on the mouthpiece. And then:

1. Slide the ligature onto the mouthpiece, holding it a bit higher than where it will eventually be positioned.
2. Slide the wet reed under the ligature. Make sure that the reed lines up with the mouthpiece, both at the tip and the sides.

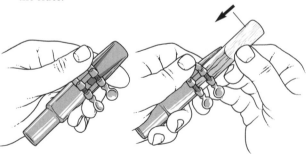

1. Just a bit higher   2. Slide the reed under the ligature.

3. Hold the mouthpiece between your thumb and index finger so that the reed stays in place, while sliding the ligature into position. Check to see that the reed is still where it's supposed to be.

4. Tighten the ligature screw(s). Not too tight, though, if you want the reed to vibrate freely. Above all, try to avoid touching the vulnerable tip of the reed at all times.

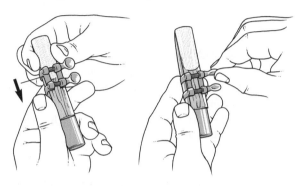

3. Slide the ligature into position... 4. ... and tighten the screw(s).

The ligature
The ligature is a bit wider at one end than at the other. The mouthpiece is too. So make sure that you put the ligature on the mouthpiece the right way around. If you think this is a silly mistake, well, it is. Yet it happens.

Twist the crook
Attach the mouthpiece to the crook, then insert the crook into the body, gently twisting it from side to side. The small screw of the crook receiver, like the ligature screws, should not be fastened too tightly. Many saxophonists don't hold their horn directly in front of them, but off to the right a bit. If this sounds like you, then swivel the crook slightly to the left, and make sure the octave mechanism is still lined up.

Warming up
A cold sax doesn't respond very well and it will sound a little flat. Warm it up by blowing a few long, slow, silent breaths through the instrument. If your sax has become very cold in transit, you can insert a small towel into the bell to speed up the process. Some players, of course, just

start playing immediately, reckoning that the instrument will warm itself up in no time.

TUNING

Everyone knows you are supposed to tune a guitar before you play it. But a sax? Yes, a sax too. Even if you're just playing by yourself a sax will only play in tune if it has been tuned properly.

Adjusting the mouthpiece

You tune a sax by simply pushing the mouthpiece further onto the crook cork or by pulling it off a little. This makes the entire instrument a bit shorter or longer and so raises or lowers the pitch. It's easy to remember: the longer the tube, the lower the pitch.

Extreme tuning

If you tune your sax extremely high or low you may have intonation problems, as the position of the tone holes won't correspond to the total length of the horn anymore. The low register will sound sloppy if the mouthpiece is too far back, as well.

The A

Just like other instruments, saxophones usually tune to a concert A. You'll find this note to the right of middle C on a well-tuned piano or other keyboard instrument. The illustration on the following page shows you the right key. A string

An A on a keyboard

sounding this A usually vibrates 440 times per second. If there isn't a keyboard instrument handy use a tuning fork. Most electronic metronomes and tuners can play this A too.

Alto and tenor sax

On an alto sax you get this note by fingering an F-sharp, with the octave key depressed. On a tenor sax you get it by fingering a B, also using the octave key.

A different pitch

Some saxophonists prefer to tune to a different pitch.

You can tune an alto sax by fingering a B, with your left index finger on key 1. This will give you a concert D. On the tenor you finger the same B, resulting in an A one octave below the standard tuning A.

Why B?

Why that B? Because it's easy to play, and because you can use your other hand to play the relevant key on the piano. Some players also feel that it's more difficult to play

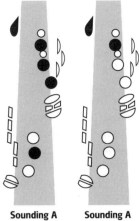

| Sounding A on an alto (fingered F♯) | Sounding A on a tenor (fingered B) |

in tune while using the octave key, so they prefer to tune without it. Others disagree. Their view is that the B without the octave key may sound slightly flat, on tenors even more so than on altos. A tip: try both ways, and see what works best for you.

HERE'S A TRICK

If you are a beginner it may be difficult to hear whether your instrument sounds too high or too low. Here's a trick: first push the mouthpiece so far onto the crook that the note is obviously sharp. Then pull it out so far that the note is obviously flat. The correct tuning will be somewhere in the middle.

Electronic tuners

Most electronic tuners have a built-in microphone that 'hears' what you play, registering it on the dial as sharp (too high), flat (too low) or just right. Tuning with such a tuner seems to make sense, but there are teachers who will ask you not to, as it doesn't help develop your ears. Cheaper tuners may respond very slowly to the sound of a sax, so they aren't of much use anyway. Try out a few models before buying one.

A warm sax

A sax will warm up with playing, so you may have to retune after a while. The warmer it gets, the higher the pitch. If it's extremely hot or freezing cold, it may be hard to get it in tune at all.

Tuning line

Is your sax warmed up and well tuned? Then draw a line on the crook cork or *tuning cork*, just where the mouthpiece ends. The next time you play, simply align the mouthpiece to this line, and you'll always be close to being in tune. This tuning line may not be of help when you're playing in a group as you are need to be in tune with the other instruments. If you have to tune to a synthesizer or another electronic keyboard instrument ask the player to use an even sound that is clear of effects.

A different mouthpiece

As mouthpieces differ in length the tuning line is not going to be much use when you're trying out mouthpieces. Just retune your sax for each new mouthpiece.

Paper, thread, or match?

If the crook cork has been so compressed that your mouthpiece doesn't fit properly any more, simply wrap a piece of paper around the cork and fit the mouthpiece over it. Cigarette paper is perfect. As an alternative you can wrap some thread around the cork, then rub it with a candle. The best solution is to have the crook recorked. If you need a quick fix and there's no paper or thread on hand then carefully warm the crook cork with a lighter, a match or a candle – and please be aware of the fact that cork burns pretty easily.

AFTERWARDS

If you don't clean your instrument and mouthpiece each time you finish playing, it will eventually start to smell a bit off-putting.

Reed care

Once you've finished playing, take the reed off the mouthpiece. Carefully dry it, using your clothes (cotton clothes work best) or a rag. Better still, first rinse the reed with water and then dry it along its length from the heel to the tip.

Reed guard

Storing your reeds in a *reed guard* protects them from damage and allows them to dry flat. A cheaper alternative is to fit some rubber bands around a piece of glass with polished edges. Small mirrors, available at chemists, work fine.

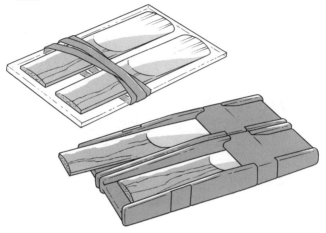

Piece of glass with rubber band, and a reed guard

On the mouthpiece

Some players just leave the (dried) reed on the mouthpiece – although this may result in a wavy tip or even in the plating coming off of a metal mouthpiece. If you do this then always use your mouthpiece cap, and if you are taking a breather then always use the cap to protect the reed and to prevent warping.

Moisture control

Some players in very dry climates store their reeds in special moisture-controlled cases, some even featuring built-in hygrometers. A less expensive alternative is to keep your reed guard in a freezer box or zip-up freezer bag, which will help to prevent the reeds drying out. Never store them in a jar of water, no matter how dry the climate is, as this would make the reeds more porous and less vibrant.

The body

When you play a wind instrument, the moisture in your breath condenses on the inside of the body. That's not anything to worry about in itself. The problem is in the pads, however, which suck up the moisture like sponges. If you don't do anything about it they will get hard and brittle, just like a pair of soaking wet leather shoes that have been put in front of a fireplace. Besides being noisy, sooner of later hard and brittle pads will start leaking.

Pad saver or swab?

What's the best way to keep your pads in good shape? Some players go for the pad saver; others swear by the swab.

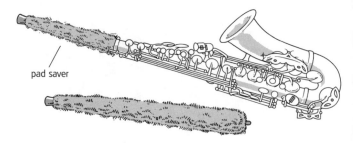

pad saver

Pad saver

A *pad saver* is a long fuzz-covered rod that you insert and pull out of your sax a couple of times after playing. This takes care of most of the moisture. Many players keep their pad saver in their instrument when they're not playing, but it's better to take it out. Then, when you get home, open the case just a bit so that the pads can dry slowly. Pad savers cost around £10/$15. Some people dislike them as they find them to be pretty dusty.

Swab

A cleaning swab is a long string with a small weight attached to one end, and a piece of chamois (soft leather), silk or cotton cloth attached to the other. Simply drop the weight down the body and pull the swab through the instrument a couple of times. Again, open the case upon returning home to allow the pads to finish drying.

End plug

The *end plug* protects the octave key rod that protrudes from the top of the body. End plugs can be made of rubber, plastic, metal, wood or cork. Simply insert it into the body before packing up.

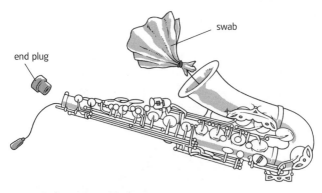

The crook and mouthpiece

There are special swabs and crook savers to rid the crook of moisture. They also clean off any other debris that may have ended up there. An ordinary handkerchief will do for your mouthpiece, but mouthpiece savers are available as well. Don't forget to dry the outside, too.

Storing your sax

Always store your sax in its case. Apart from the risk of it being kicked or tripped over, if you don't the pads will dry out too much, and airborne dust may clog the key system. Should you have to leave your saxophone uncovered for any extended period, always make sure it's kept out of the sun and not near any source of heat.

Dishcloth

There are inexpensive and high quality pouches designed for mouthpieces and crooks, but most sax players simply wrap them up in an old dishcloth or a rag. Pick one that doesn't shed a lot of lint, and wrap up the crook and mouthpiece separately to keep them from damaging each other.

Cases and gig bags

Never travel without a good case, for which you can expect to pay £50–200/$75–250. Cases and gig bags come in all qualities and types. In addition to the traditional rectangular type, there are cases formed to the shape of the horn. The best-protected hard cases are usually referred to as *flight case*, designed to prevent damage if the instrument has to be transported in the hold of an aeroplane. A *gig bag* is a soft case.

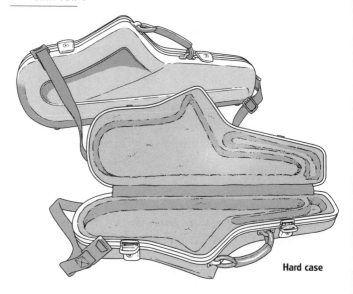

Hard case

A few tips

- Good cases and bags have sturdy, well-attached handles and shoulder straps. Latches shouldn't come open spontaneously.
- A plush lining will protect your instrument from scratches.
- Check for a perfect fit, so that nothing gets bent or shifts around in transit.
- If a case is too small, keys that should stay closed may be pressed open, and vice versa.
- Hard-shell cases are less comfortable to carry then soft-shell cases, but offer more protection.
- Gig bags and flight cases are easier to transport than rectangular cases.
- Rectangular cases have more storage room.
- Smaller cases seem to have no room for the crook. The solution is to simply stick it in the bell. Wrap it up, first.
- No car? Get a backpack-model case or bag.
- Compartments or outside pockets are handy for stashing extra reeds, a second mouthpiece, a neck strap, music, books, or even a music stand.

AND WHAT'S MORE

As a sax player you've also got to deal with neck straps and stands, perhaps even with microphones and amplifiers.

Neck straps

The most basic neck straps or *slings* can get very uncomfortable after a while. If you want something better, then have a look at wider straps with comfortable padding, and for the type of strap that sits low on your shoulders rather than on your neck. Straps with an elastic back are also available. Some players like them because of their flexible feel. Others don't, because of their flexible feel.

Harness

If you want to avoid putting a strain on your neck entirely, buy a *harness*, which fits over your shoulders and around your waist. It's a bit of a nuisance to get into, and not everyone feels it enhances their stage image, but it's very comfortable. Harnesses or *dual shoulder straps* are particularly advisable for younger players. A variation on the harness employs braces that you fasten to the rear belt loops of your trousers.

A regular neck strap, a brace, and a harness

Hooks

Pay some attention to the hook, too. Many players go for the most straightforward type (basically a bent piece of hardened steel wire). A soft coating keeps this type of hook from scratching your instrument.

Spring hooks

Other hooks employ some kind of spring action. They're usually considered to be more secure, but they take more time when changing instruments. Some of these hooks can swivel around freely so the neck strap doesn't get twisted.

Support

There are good hooks and bad hooks. The bad ones can break (watch out for cheap plastic ones), open inadvertently,

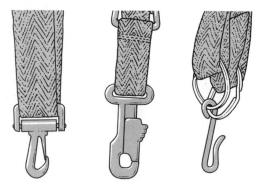

A spring hook, a snap hook and a simple hook

or allow the sax to work itself loose. An important tip: don't allow the sax to swing loose, but always support it with one hand, even when you're not playing and however reliable you think your hook is.

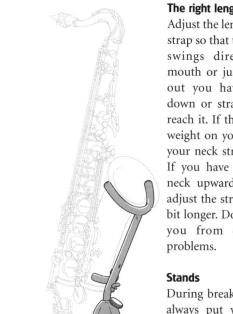

Basic sax stand
(adjustable for tenor or alto)

The right length

Adjust the length of the neck strap so that the mouthpiece swings directly to your mouth or just below, without you having to stoop down or strain upwards to reach it. If there's too much weight on your thumb then your neck strap is too long. If you have to strain your neck upward to play, then adjust the strap so that it's a bit longer. Do it. It may save you from chronic neck problems.

Stands

During breaks from playing always put your sax on a stand. Good sax stands have soft bumpers and long legs for stability, they are sturdy, easily collapsible, and easy to transport. Prices start at about £20/$25. An additional safety tip: use gaffer tape/duct tape to fasten the stand to the floor so it won't get knocked over.

Lyre
Marching sax players can attach a music stand to their instruments. Most saxes have a small clamp for these so-called *lyres*, which come in many different versions, some very basic, others with well-designed wind and rain resistant features.

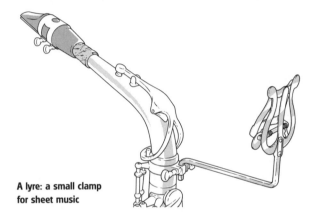

A lyre: a small clamp for sheet music

AMPLIFICATION
A sax can play pretty loud, but not as loud as many other instruments. Trying to compete is tiring and it's hard to get a good sound and play in tune if you really have to blast away. Amplification is the answer.

Microphones
Most good vocal microphones work well for saxophones as well. Using a traditional microphone on a stand has one disadvantage: you have to constantly aim your sound directly at it. One solution is to use a small clip-on microphone that attaches to the bell, allowing you to move around more freely. Prices run from £140 to £350/$200 to $500. Cordless systems are usually more expensive.

Amplifiers and effects
Sax players use far fewer electronic effects than electric guitarists do, but the use of a *reverb* and a *delay* is quite

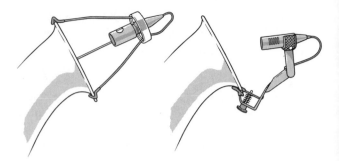

Sax microphones, mounted on the bell of the instrument (SD Systems)

common, and a *flanger*, a *chorus* or a *wahwah* can be fun to experiment with. If you always play amplified, it's not a bad idea to buy your own gear. A keyboard amplifier works well for general use.

Two more safety tips:

- Note down the serial number of your instrument, preferably before it's stolen or lost. There's space to do so on page 116. You'll usually find this number under the thumb hook, or on or near the bell.
- Consider insuring your instrument, especially if you take it on the road – which includes visiting your teacher. Musical instruments fall under the insurance category of 'valuables'. A regular home insurance policy will not cover all possible damage, whether it occurs at home, on the road, in the studio, or on stage.

10. CLEANING AND MAINTENANCE

If you follow the tips in the preceding chapter conscientiously your saxophone will require little further maintenance. Likewise, there won't be any great need to do much doctoring of the instrument yourself. For the most part it's better to leave this to a specialist repairer, just like the periodic check-ups and adjustments. Still, here is a handful of additional tips to help you keep your instrument clean and in optimum working condition.

A soft, dry or slightly damp lint-free cloth and a small brush for tricky places are all you need to clean dust from the body of your horn. If you don't do so occasionally, dust may build up in the hinges, resulting in a slower action and, eventually, excessive wear of the key system. It's not a bad idea to vacuum your case once in a while, for the same reason. When cleaning the instrument, be careful not to prick your fingers on the sharp ends of the springs under the keys.

No polish
Never use any kind of metal polish on your sax. It eats away the lacquer if there is any, and gets into the hinges, gumming up the key system, and onto the pads. On silver-plated saxes you may, very carefully, use a silver-polishing cloth once in while.

Your mouthpiece
It's good to wash your mouthpiece with warm water every now and then. Adding a small amount of diluted vinegar helps avoid the build-up of scale – and scale may very well hold some disagreeable residues. Never leave a hard rubber

mouthpiece in hot water or a vinegar solution. It won't fall apart, but it will become discoloured. Don't use any harsh detergents or cleaning fluids on them, either. You can use rubbing alcohol to disinfect a mouthpiece.

Swab and pad saver

Swabs and pad savers pick up a lot of muck from your horn, so launder them from time to time and let them dry thoroughly before using them again. Warm water and a mild detergent will do.

Sticking pads

Pads can stick, and especially the pads that are closed when at rest. To correct this, stick a piece of ordinary paper, a handkerchief or a lens cleaning cloth under the pad, and close the key a few times. If that doesn't do the trick, try carefully pulling the piece of paper or cloth out from under the pad while you keep it gently closed, your finger on the cup. If it keeps sticking it's best to have the pad replaced.

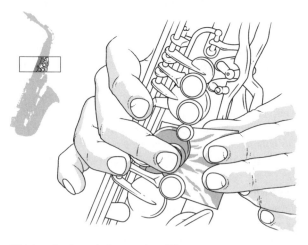

Stick it under the pad, close gently, pull it out

Currency notes and talcum powder

A currency note may work even better than plain paper, as it has a rough surface. Cigarette paper is fine, too. It's best to avoid using paper tissues, as they may fall apart or get stuck. Another trick is to apply a bit of talcum powder to the pad with a cotton bud or an old reed.

The tenons

The top part of the body is the *receiver tenon*, which 'receives' the *crook tenon* when assembling the horn. Keeping the tenons clean with a little white spirit or rubbing alcohol helps to get the crook in smoothly. Lacquer hates alcohol, so don't spill any.

Cork grease

Smear a bit of *cork grease* on the crook cork, from time to time. It keeps the cork from disintegrating spontaneously, eases putting the mouthpiece on the crook and provides a good seal.

On the road

There are a few tips that may help you when you're having troubles on the road, and there's no repairman around.

- If a key suddenly stops working, then have a look at the corresponding spring. If it turns out to have disappeared altogether, a rubber band may help. Has the spring simply come loose? Replace it where it should be. A crochet needle is a useful tool for this purpose. Always remove the rubber band after playing as it may start to perish and damage your horn if you leave it on for too long.
- Lost your low register? The chances are that the crook octave vent is not closing. This may require some serious and very careful bending of the octave mechanism, a job you may want to leave to your repairer.
- Too much noise? Check for missing felts and corks. You can reglue them with a drop of water-soluble glue. Other types of glue may harden your felts, spoil your finish, or be so permanent that felts and corks can't be replaced anymore.
- Don't just replace a missing felt with any piece of felt. Not every piece of felt is suitable for this purpose, and the thickness is critical too.
- Squeaks? Wet the reed. Replace the reed. Practice more.

CHECK-UP

A periodic check-up involves a thorough inspection and adjustment of the entire instrument. A general guideline is that if you play anything from four to eight hours a week, have your horn checked once a year.

Sneaky leaks

Most leaks arrive gradually. So gradually, in fact, you may not even notice them coming. You'll just find yourself beginning to squeeze the keys and blowing harder and harder. Have a fellow player give your instrument a try once in a while. They may be able to spot sneaky leaks that you haven't noticed yet, since they haven't adjusted their technique to cope with them.

The costs

If you play a few times a week and take good care of your horn, an annual check-up and adjustment will cost around £20–30/$25–50. If you play more often, decide to ignore the advice in this book altogether, or if you're used to blowing huge amounts of drinks and food through your instrument, then the price may be higher. Some music shops and repair workshops may provide you with a loan instrument while yours is in the shop. It pays to check this in advance.

Overhaul

An overhaul includes everything that needs to be done. All the keys will be removed, dents will be fixed, the horn will be cleaned, all pads, corks and felts will be replaced, and the key system will be replaced, oiled and adjusted. How often your instrument needs an overhaul depends, among other things, on how much you play and on how much you do to keep your instrument in good working order. The costs of such an operation are usually between £120–£350/$200–$600. For more money you can have your instrument stripped, buffed and refinished with lacquer or plating, depending on the instrument.

11. BACK IN TIME

Not many musical instruments have been named after their inventor, simply because most instruments were not invented but developed over time. The saxophone is one of the few exceptions. Instrument maker Adolphe Sax is best known for his saxophone, but he also invented percussion instruments, a host of other wind instruments, including curiosities like the *saxtromba*, and even some medical equipment. The *Sax-o-phone* is the only one of his inventions to have really caught on.

Ophicleide

There are many stories about what Sax was really after when working on the saxophone, but only one is correct: he wanted to create an instrument with the power of a brass wind instrument, the virtuoso possibilities and the flexibility of a string instrument, and the timbre of a woodwind instrument. One of his main inspirations was the *ophicleide* or keyed bugle, a now obsolete instrument with a woodwind key system and a trumpet-like mouthpiece.

Nine saxophones

Sax built his first Sax-o-phone around 1840. The range of that instrument was similar to that of the modern baritone sax. A couple of years later he had built four different saxes, and in the following years he completed the others. They didn't get their names until around 1855. In all, Sax introduced nine different saxophones. Some sources mention twelve or even fourteen models; as Sax gave his instruments their final names long after their creation, there is some confusion as to the identities of the instruments.

Adolphe Sax (1814–94)

Success

Five of Sax's saxes were intended for use in military bands, where they were more than welcome. The others were created with the symphony orchestra in mind. This was less of a success, as these orchestras were not awaiting this new instrument with bated breath. One good reason? There wasn't any music written for it yet.

Alone and a pauper

It was only much later that the saxophone began to find a place in the world of classical music, with interest from composers growing only tentatively. It was jazz musicians who were to make the sax really popular, when jazz began to develop at the beginning of the twentieth century. Too late for Adolphe Sax, unfortunately: he died in 1894, alone and a pauper.

12. THE SAX FAMILY

To call the various saxophones members of a 'family' is a bit of a misnomer. They are just different voices of a single instrument of the woodwind family. The *woodwind* family? Saxes are made of brass, so surely they must be brass instruments? Well, no, they're not. Here's a brief guide to some of the variations of the saxophone as well as an introduction to some other woodwinds and electronic wind instruments.

Do saxes count as woodwind instruments because the first saxes used a wooden mouthpiece, or because the reed is made of 'wood'? No. Saxophones are considered woodwind

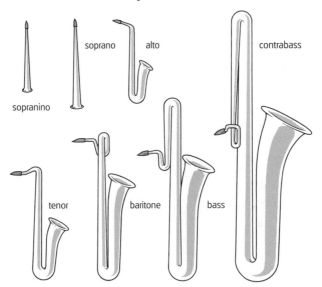

instruments because their means of sound production is like that of most other members of that family. The sound of a sax resembles that of a clarinet far more than it does that of a brass instrument such as the trumpet, and to a great extent this is because they both produce it by means of a vibrating reed rather than by applying the lips direct to a mouthpiece.

Sopranino

Bass saxophone

A family portrait

The four most important types of saxophone are described in chapter 3, *Four Saxes*. You don't see the others very often. The sopranino is smaller and therefore even higher in pitch than the soprano. The bass saxophone is an octave lower than the tenor, and the contrabass is an octave lower than the baritone.

Straight and curved

The most common soprano and sopranino models are straight in shape, but some makers offer curved models too. Conversely, straight altos and tenors are also available.

In C

When you finger a C on the tenor sax, you hear a B-flat. At some point someone felt the need for a non-transposing sax and invented the *C-Melody* or *C tenor*: a saxophone that sounds at concert pitch. Seemed like a good idea, but it never caught on. Although C-Melody saxes were

A straight alto sax

popular in the Twenties – you can often hear them in the sax sections of dance bands from that era – they eventually went out of fashion.

Nowadays it's very hard to find reeds, mouthpieces or other parts for them. The same goes for the mezzo-soprano sax in F, the soprano sax in C, the sopranino in F, and for the *saxello*: a soprano sax in B-flat, its bell pointing towards the audience, built in the Twenties.

Flute

Although not a reed instrument, the flute is a woodwind instrument too; the first flutes were made of wood. Wooden flutes are still in production but the vast majority are made of metal. Because the key systems of the flute and saxophone are so similar, quite a few people play both instruments.

Flute   **Clarinet**   **Oboe**

Clarinet

That's also true for the clarinet, which has a similar mouthpiece to the sax. Still, there are considerable differences
between the two. A clarinet has a cylindrical (straight)
bore, a number of tone holes are closed by the fingertips

(instead of pads), the system of fingering is different, and it requires a different embouchure and air stream – so there's quite a bit to adjust to.

Oboe

The oboe, like the sax, has a conical bore but its wooden body and key system are closer to that of the clarinet. In addition it's a double-reed instead of a single-reed instrument; it has two reeds that vibrate against each other, just as do the bassoon and the English horn.

Electronic wind instruments

The Lyricon, Akai's EWI and the Yamaha WX are electronic wind instruments that have been developed taking the saxophone as a basic model. You can think of them as saxophone synthesizers with an almost unlimited array of sounds. Their breath control, which they share with the sax, offers a type of expressiveness unavailable to keyboard synths. Since they have their own system of fingering and a number of features enabled by their electronic status they do take some time to learn. The Synthophone, an alto sax with electronic sensors on the keys, has the same possibilities as these other 'horns' but it offers the experienced saxophonist a more familiar fingering system.

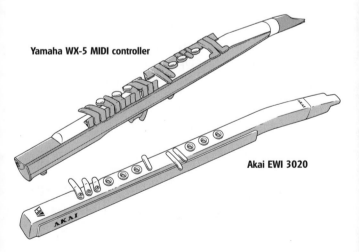

Yamaha WX-5 MIDI controller

Akai EWI 3020

13. HOW THEY'RE MADE

How is a sax built, what kinds of machines are used to make mouthpieces, and where do reeds come from? Here's quick look at some of the various processes used in saxophone manufacture.

The main part of the body is produced from a sheet of brass, which is made into a 'flat' tube. This tube is usually given its round shape using dies and mechanical presses. Modern techniques have gradually been taking over from the traditional process, which used a wooden hammer to shape the tube around a die.

Two halves

The bell and the bow are made in approximately the same way. You have to search pretty hard to find the seam, as polishing can almost completely erase any visible signs. The crook is in essence a bent length of pipe. How do you bend a pipe without it buckling? In this case you fill it with water or a soap solution, allow it to freeze, and then set about the work.

The traditional way: shaping the tube with a wooden hammer

The tone holes

Before the tone holes are made, smaller holes are drilled in the body and the bell at the correct places. Next a metal shaft is inserted into the body. This *spike* is inset with metal balls, each one exactly matching the size of the corresponding tone hole. These balls are pulled forcibly through the pre-drilled holes, so creating tone holes of the correct size.

Posts

Once the body is finished, the posts that hold the rods and keys in place are soldered onto it. Soldering individual posts to the body is called *mounting* them. In the case of saxes with a rib or ribbed construction a series of posts is soldered onto metal strips that are then attached to the body.

Testing and adjusting

Once all the parts have been polished and lacquered, the bell engraved and the pads seated, the sax is ready for assembly. At the end of the process, it will be tested and adjusted. Most new saxes, however, need an extra adjustment in the store before they're really ready to play.

REEDS AND MOUTHPIECES

You might feel that reeds are quite expensive for what are, after all, just simple pieces of cane. One reason for the high cost is that manufacturers can only use about a quarter of the cane they buy. The rest is simply discarded. Another is that making a reed is quite a time-consuming job.

Arundo Donax

Reeds are cut from *Arundo Donax*, a long hollow cane closely related to bamboo. Most of it comes from the south of France (the Var region), but it grows in other Mediterranean countries, in South America and in California as well.

Ageing and curing

The plants are ready for harvesting when they're two to three years old and about twenty-five feet high. Between harvesting and making the reed a substantial period of time elapses: the cane needs to be cured for a year or more before it can be made into a sax reed.

The shape

The tubes of cane, sorted for size and cut to length, are split lengthways into four pieces. A variety of steps follow, from making the rough shape to a finished reed. Reeds are shaved to an accuracy of half a thousandth of an inch. The final step for every reed is to be graded for strength. A reed's strength is not based on its thickness, but on its hardness. This is done with very simple hand-operated devices that determine the hardness by just bending the tip of the reed a little to measure the resistance of the cane.

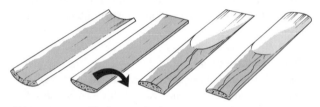

From cane to reed, in four very basic steps

Mouthpieces

Mouthpieces are either cast or begin as solid blocks of material that are given a rough shape by lathes and milling machines. Diamond cutting tools with tolerances of tens of thousandths of an inch are often used for the final adjustment of the facing, although hand facing is still quite common, too. The cheapest plastic mouthpieces are made by injecting plastic into a mould, creating the basic shape in one quick process. The facings are then made by machine.

14. THE BRANDS

The sax has become increasingly popular in recent years, and a large number of brands are available. In fact, there are more brands than there are factories. This chapter briefly describes some of the most important names, and also introduces some examples of vintage horns.

To offer a complete discussion of the various brands would require an entire book, mainly because it's a fairly involved business. There are manufacturers who build saxes for a number of separate brands, while other brands included – or still do – instruments made by different manufacturers, while in the case of Selmer there is a single brand name but two separate companies – French and American.

B&S, in former East Germany, build saxes in all price ranges. The company made and still makes budget instruments under a variety of national and international brands such as Sonora, Weltklang and Bandmaster. They also make higher quality, both under the B&S and other names.

The first Buffet Crampon saxophones were made in 1868, just two years after Adolphe Sax's patent had expired. These higher-priced French instruments are mostly intended for classical musicians. A line of more affordable Taiwanese-made saxes is marketed as the Buffet Crampon Evette.

 The German company Julius Keilwerth, founded in 1925, produces instruments in the mid-to-high price range. Keilwerth has always made instruments for other brands as well. Two examples are Couf and Armstrong, both from the States.

 Selmer has long been the largest manufacturer of saxophones for professional and semi-professional use. The first Selmers were made in France in 1922. Six years later, Selmer bought the brand name Adolphe Sax Fils (Adolphe Sax Junior). Selmer established its name in America before World War II, at which time the firm worked together with Buescher.

Selmer® The American Selmer company evolved from the French collaboration with Buescher. Though they share the same name, American and French Selmer are now separate and independent companies. Selmer USA manufacture saxophones in the lower price range, using the names Selmer Bundy and Selmer Signet.

YAMAHA In addition to saxophones, Yamaha make drums, pianos, synthesizers, boats and motorcycles and other items. It is one of the few sax makers to offer instruments in all price categories, from student to professional models. The first Yamaha saxes appeared on the market in 1967.

YANAGISAWA Yanagisawa began its production of saxophones in 1954. At present they only make instruments in the higher price range. Of particular interest are the models with solid silver crooks and bells. The Japanese factory also manufactures crooks in a variety of materials for other brands.

New American saxes

For a long time America, next to France, was the country that produced the best saxophones. In the Sixties things changed. Japanese manufacturers took over the American market, producing less expensive saxophones of an acceptable quality. Most new American-made saxes are now in the lower price range, costing up to £600/$1000. Conn and King, now daughter companies of UMI (United Musical Instruments), and Leblanc are three examples. The slightly more expensive saxes of L.A. Sax are available in pretty much any colour and design, from fire engine red to Siberian Tiger.

Taiwan and others

After the Japanese conquest, it was Taiwan's turn to enter saxophone production, with instruments priced up to about £700/$1000. In recent years these instruments have noticeably improved. Well-known brands are Dixon and Jupiter, both brand names of large companies that produce a wide range of other instruments, from drums to trumpets. Inexpensive saxes are made in other Asian countries as well, usually based on popular designs by other brands.

Other names

Many of the above-mentioned saxes can be found under a variety of names. Keep in mind that prices can vary radically; the same sax may cost much less as Brand A than as Brand B.

Other countries

There are, of course, many other brands of saxophone from other countries. The Czech Amati, for example, which also makes many saxes for other companies. Italy has Grassi, Borgani and Orsi among others. The last co-operates closely with L.A. Sax. Instruments by Trevor James ('The Horn') come from England and Taiwan, Weril from Brazil, and Pearl from Japan.

VINTAGE SAXES

Vintage saxes built around or before the early Sixties may be quite valuable. Some models, of course, had good and bad years. Well-equipped music shops have listings of serial numbers, so you can find out exactly when a sax was

CHAPTER 14

built. These listings can also be found on the Internet (see *Want to know more?* on page 113).

Old American horns
Pretty much every 'old' American sax maker produced one or more horns that are still in demand.
- Conn, for instance, founded in 1888 as the first American sax manufacturer, became best known for the Ladyface, the Conquerer and the Chu Berry.
- King's claims to fame were the Zephyr and the Super 20, among others.
- Ferdinand August Buescher, who first worked for Conn, later produced his own instruments. The 400 and the Aristocrat are famous models.
- Martin was known for its soldered tone holes. The Committee and the Magna are some of the best known models of this brand. Martin also made a sax with mother-of-pearl side keys, known as the Typewriter.

Selmer
Well-known vintage Selmers are the Super Action and the Balanced Action. Their key mechanisms, compared to American-made saxes from that period, were quite advanced. The most famous sax of all time is probably the Selmer Mark VI, of which the best were produced during the Fifties. A good Mark VI will easily cost £2000/$3000 or more.

Appreciation
In order to fetch a high price a horn needs to be in good condition, or should at least be in good enough condition to be restored to its former glory. Don't worry about the lacquer – if there's any left, that is. The money you invest in such a sax is usually a sound investment; good horns may appreciate in value as they get older.

Old for less
Other older instruments offer reasonable quality for less money. A few examples from the late Fifties until the late Seventies are the Martin Handcraft, the King Cleveland, the Selmer Bundy, the Conn PanAm and the Conn USA. It's impossible to quote exact prices, but a rough figure for such an instrument is in the range £700 to £1000/$1000 to $1250.

And still less

Even if you are a beginner and don't want to pay more than £750/$1000 or so for a used instrument, there are older instruments around that may answer your needs. There are plenty of good, affordable instruments made around the late Seventies, for instance by Armstrong and Vito. The King 613 and the Conn 16M also belong to this category.

VINTAGE MOUTHPIECES

There's also a market for certain older mouthpieces, some of which are highly sought after by players who want a traditional, vintage sound. Otto Links from the Fifties are now worth £150/$200, as are Dukoffs from the Forties, and Brilhart mouthpieces – the ones Charlie Parker played on – from the Forties and Fifties are gaining popularity as well. A tip: just as new mouthpieces don't always work well with vintage saxophones, old mouthpieces may not suit new horns either.

GLOSSARY AND INDEX

This glossary contains short definitions of all saxophone-related terms used in this book. There are also some words you won't find on the previous pages, but which you might well come across in magazines, catalogues and books. Page numbers refer to the pages where the term is used in this book.

Action *(37–38)* The mechanical 'feel' of your sax, mostly influenced by the adjustment of springs and keys.

Adjustment *(26, 38, 76–77, 87–88, 97)* The process of fiddling with keys, corks, pads etc so that an instrument plays at its best.

Altissimo register *(34)* Also known as top tones or high harmonics: these are high notes produced by special techniques of fingering and reed control that are above the normal register of the instrument.

Alto saxophone *(13)* One of the two most widely-played saxes.

American cut *(64)* A reed with a slightly thicker tip and less heart, as opposed to French cut. See also: *French cut, French file cut.*

Articulated C-sharp *(35)* System that closes the C-sharp pad when low B or B-flat is played.

Articulated G-sharp, Automatic G-sharp *(34–35)* Opens the G-sharp pad when low C-sharp, B or B-flat are played.

Automatic octave key See: *Octave key, octave vents.*

Baffle *(51, 57)* A 'bump' on the inside of the mouthpiece, providing a more aggressive, piercing sound.

Baritone saxophone *(15)* The lowest sounding of the four most common sax models.

Bell *(3–5)* The flared opening of the sax.

Bend See: *Bow.*

Body *(3–6, 43, 96)* The main segment of the saxophone, not including the crook or mouthpiece.

Bore *(43)* The internal shape of the body. A mouthpiece has a bore, too, like any other tubular item.

Bow *(3, 4, 96)* The curved part between the body of the sax and the bell. Also called the bend.

Brace 1. Connects the body and the bell; often a metal ring (circular brace). 2. A type of neck strap.

Brass *(30, 43)* Alloy of copper and zinc, the most common material used for saxophones.

Button key See: *Keys.*

Cap *(77)* Used to protect reed and mouthpiece.

Carborundum stone See: *Whetstone.*

Cases and gig bags *(79–80)* Means of carrying a sax about, providing a greater or lesser amount of protection.

Chamber *(50–51, 57)* The internal space of a mouthpiece.

Check-ups *(87–88)* Take the instrument to a specialist every so often to ensure that everything is still working properly.

Concert A concert B-flat is the standard B-flat – that on a piano keyboard, for

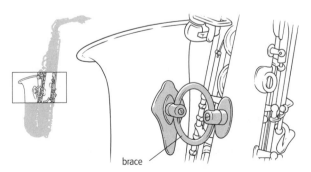

brace

The brace: the supporting piece of metal between the body and the bell

Dutch rush

example. On a tenor sax you finger a C to get a *sounding* or concert B-flat. See: *Transposing instruments.*

Conical bore *(6, 95)* A sax has a conical bore, narrow at the top and getting wider towards the bell, just like a cone. See also: *Bore.*

Cork grease *(87)* Lubricant for the crook cork.

Corks *(6, 36, 87, 110)* Small corks and felts ensure that the keys open just the right amount, and that certain keys open or close simultaneously. They also keep the noise of the key system down. See also: *Crook cork.*

Crook *(4, 6, 46, 61–62, 73)* The tube that connects mouthpiece and body. Called the *neck* or *neck pipe* in the USA.

Crook cork *(46, 74, 76, 87)* Cork sleeve at the end of the crook. Also referred to as *tuning cork.*

Crook octave vent *(6, 61)* The upper octave vent. See: *Octave key, octave vent.*

Doubling Playing more

than one instrument. Many sax players double on clarinet and/or flute.

Dutch rush *(68)* A plant that grows in swamps, used for adjusting reeds. Also known as *reed rush.*

Ebonite See: *Hard rubber.*

Embouchure *(19, 50, 59, 95)* Your embouchure is the way in which you hold and flex your lips, tongue, jaw and facial muscles when playing a wind instrument.

End plug *(78)* Used when the instrument is being transported to replace the crook and protect the rod that activates the upper part of the octave mechanism.

Engraving *(31)* The bell is often engraved.

Facing *(50, 51, 53, 54, 56)* The area where the mouthpiece curves away from the reed. Also called the *lay.*

Felts *(6, 36, 38, 87)* See: *Corks.*

Fingering chart *(11)* Shows which keys to use for each note.

Forked F See: *Front F*.

French cut *(64)* French cut reeds are mainly used by classical players, and have a relatively thin tip and a slightly thicker heart area. See: *American cut*.

French file cut *(65)* Special way of cutting reeds to produce a more open, brighter sound. Not be confused with *French cut*. Also see: *American cut*.

Front F *(11, 36)* A key to assist in reaching a high E, F or F-sharp. Also referred to as *quick F* or *forked F*.

Gold lacquer *(30)* Lacquer with a golden tint.

Hard rubber *(58–69)* What most mouthpieces are made of. Also known as *ebonite*.

Heart *(69)* The backbone of a reed.

High F-sharp *(11, 33–34)* Special key to play high F-sharp.

High G *(34)* Special key to play high G, only found on a few sopranos.

High harmonics See: *Altissimo register*.

High pitch *(47)* Some older saxes were made to play at a higher standard pitch.

Hook 1. *(81)* The hook on the neck sling. 2. The supporting hook for your right thumb.

Insurance *(84)* A good idea.

Intonation *(40–42)* A sax with bad intonation will be difficult, perhaps impossible, to play in tune. A player with bad intonation will play out of tune even on the best saxophone.

Key cup *(5, 8, 38)* The cup holding the pad that covers the tone hole.

Key guards *(4, 6)* Protects the key system and keeps your clothes from getting caught in it.

Key height *(48,41)* The distance a key opens.

Key risers *(36)* Pieces of plastic or rubber to raise keys that are set too low for your hands.

Key system *(33–38)* The sax's mechanism, including keys, rods, springs and other parts.

Keys *(3–5, 7–11, 30, 33–36, 38, 46, 49)* The 'fingers' of

THE ROUGH GUIDE TO SAXOPHONE

your horn. The word *key* is often used to indicate the entire mechanism, from the part you actually operate to the key cup that covers the tone hole.

Lacquer *(30, 44–45)* Most saxes are finished with a transparent lacquer.

Lay See: *Facing length.*

Leaks *(28, 41–42, 46, 88)* A leaky sax doesn't respond well and will probably play out of tune, too.

Ligature *(4, 5, 62, 73)* Holds the reed in place.

Little finger keys *(4, 8, 9, 10)* The keys or *touch plates* that are operated with your left and right little fingers are also referred to as *plateau keys*, or *table keys*. The two groups of keys are known as *plateaux* or *tables*. Also known as *pinkie keys*.

Microphone *(83–84)* Vocal microphones are usually fine for sax players. There are also dedicated sax mikes that clip onto the bell of the instrument.

Mouthpiece *(4, 5, 39, 49, 50–61, 74–75, 77, 85–86, 97–98)* A crucial part of your sax, as it's here that the fundamental sound is produced.

Mouthpiece cushion, pad or patch *(59)* Small piece of soft material used to minimize the vibration of a (metal) mouthpiece against your teeth.

Mute *(21)* Saxophone mutes are available, but insulating your practice room has more effect.

Neck See: *Crook.*

Neck strap See: *Sling.*

Nickel *(31)* Nickel-plated saxes have a shinier finish than silver-plated ones. Modern nickel-plated saxes are often finished in black nickel.

Octave key, octave vents *(4, 6, 11, 49, 75)* The octave key 'automatically' opens the lower or the upper octave vents, depending on the note you finger. Also referred to as the *register key.*

Old saxes See: *Vintage saxes.*

Pad saver *(78, 86)* A long rod covered in absorbent material used to soak up the moisture in your instrument after playing.

Pads *(5, 38–39, 78, 85–86)* Mostly leather-covered felt discs that seal the tone holes.

Palm keys *(9)* Set of keys operated with the palm or the fingers of your left hand. See also: *Side keys.*

Pearls, pearl keys *(4, 8)* See: *Keys.*

Pinkie keys See: *Little finger keys.*

Plateau, plateau keys See: *Little finger keys.*

Post mounting *(32, 97)* Mounting the posts directly to the body, as opposed to a ribbed construction. See: *Rib construction.*

Posts *(32)* Hold the key mechanism in place.

Quick F See: *Front F.*

Rails *(51, 58, 59–60)* The edges of the window of a mouthpiece.

Range *(15)* The distance from the lowest to the highest notes of a sax. See also: *Altissimo register.*

Reed *(4, 5, 55, 69, 63–71, 72–73, 76–77, 97–98)* A piece of cane fitted to the mouthpiece that vibrates when blown to produce a note.

Reed adjustment *(68–70)* Dull, squeaking, shrill, or

uneven reeds may be adjusted, instead of rejected.

Reed clipper, reed trimmer *(68)* Tool to cut and adjust split or otherwise unsatisfactory reeds.

Reed guard *(77)* Protective holder for reeds. Also called reed case, reed holder.

Reed rush See: *Dutch rush.*

Register *(11)* The range of the saxophone is often broken down into three registers: low (notes played without the octave key), middle (with octave key), and high (with octave key plus side keys).

Register key See: *Octave key.*

Repadding Replacing pads.

Resonator *(5, 39)* Metal or plastic disc on the inside of a pad.

Rib construction, ribbed construction *(32–33, 97)* A sax on which the posts are soldered onto a strip of metal which in turn is soldered to the body, has a ribbed construction. See also: *Post mounting.*

Rocker *(9)* One of the many names for certain types of keys.

Rollers *(9, 37)* Allow your little fingers to slide from one key to the other with ease.

Sax, Adolphe 1814–94 *(89–90)* The main man, inventor of the saxophone.

Side keys *(4, 9, 35–36)* Set of keys on the lower right-hand side of the instrument, used to play high notes and trills. See also: *Palm keys.*

Side rails See: *Rails.*

Silver *(30)* Some saxes are finished with silver plating.

Sling *(81–83)* The saxophone is hooked into a sling around the neck to help support it. They come in various shapes and sizes, from a simple cord to a complicated harness. Also known as *neck strap.*

Soprano saxophone *(12)* The highest pitched of the four most common saxes. Curved sopranos *(62)* look like baby altos.

Spatula keys *(4, 9, 36)* See: *Keys.*

Springs *(6, 37, 45, 87)* A number of needle-like springs ensure that the keys return to their original positions after you've played them.

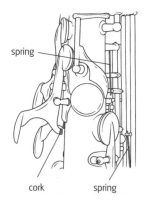

spring

cork   spring

Squeaking *(25, 57, 66, 67, 69)* Blame it on your reed, on your mouthpiece – or on yourself.

Stack To indicate the various parts of the key system the terms *low* and *high stack* are frequently used, unfortunately in a wild variety of ways. One that makes sense is to assume that every key, key cup and rod (etc) that affects the tone holes on the lower part of the body belongs to the low stack, and vice versa.

Star *(54)* A 5* mouthpiece (a 'five star') plays heavier than a straight number 5.

Strap See: *Sling.*

Swab *(78, 86)* Cotton, silk or chamois rag attached to a string and a small weight which is pulled through the instrument after playing.

Table 1. *(51)* The flat part

of the mouthpiece. 2. *(63)* The flat underside of the reed. 3. The two groups of little finger keys. See: *Little finger keys.*

Tenor saxophone *(13–15)* One of the two most commonly played saxes.

Thumb hook, thumb rest *(4, 6, 37)* Thumb hooks (right thumb) help support the instrument and may be adjustable. Thumb rests (left thumb) are small pieces of plastic which support the thumb, and aren't.

Thumb saver *(37)* A soft sleeve to cover the thumb hook.

Tip opening *(51, 53, 54, 55–56)* The distance between the tip of the reed and the tip of the mouthpiece.

Tip rail See: *Rails.*

Tone holes *(3–5, 32, 41, 74)* The holes in the sax, also called sound holes or vents.

Touch plates See: *Little finger keys.*

Transposing instruments *(15, 16)* The saxophone is a transposing instrument; the C on an alto sax sounds an E-flat on the piano, and

the C on a tenor sax sounds a B-flat.

Trill keys *(49)* Special keys enabling you to play fast trills with less trouble.

Tuning *(60, 74–77)* Adjusting the position of the mouthpiece so that the instrument plays at the correct pitch. Saxes need to be tuned, and not only when they're being played in an ensemble.

Tuning cork See: *Crook cork.*

Tuning line *(76)* Tune your sax, and draw a line on the cork, exactly where the mouthpiece ends. Lining up mouthpiece and tuning line gets you in the general vicinity of 'in tune'.

Used instruments *(26–27, 44–49)* Buying a used instrument may be a bargain, or it may not.

Vintage saxes *(26–27, 48–49, 89–90, 101–103)* Good vintage saxes, many produced in the late Fifties and early Sixties, are much in demand.

Warming-up *(73, 75–76)* A cold instrument needs to be warmed up by blowing air through it.

Wedge See: *Baffle*.

Whetstone *(68)* Tool to help adjusting reeds. Also known as carborundum stone.

Window *(51)* The open part of the mouthpiece.

Woodwind instrument *(91–93)* Saxophones are considered woodwind instruments, even though they are made of metal, because of the fingering system and because they produce their sound from a vibrating reed.

WANT TO KNOW MORE?

This book gives you all the basics you need for buying, maintaining and using a saxophone. If you want to know more, try the magazines, books, Web sites and newsgroups listed below.

MAGAZINES

- *The Saxophone Journal* is the only magazine dedicated entirely to the saxophone, and features interviews, articles, charts and more. For more information: Dorn Publications Inc., P.O. Box 206, Medfield, MA 02052, phone (508) 359-1015, fax (508) 359-7988, www.dornpub.com, dornpub@dornpub.com.
- *Windplayer* is an American magazine covering all wind instruments and a wide variety of styles. For more information: Windplayer Publications, P.O. Box 2750, Malibu, CA 90265, phone (310) 456-5813, fax (310) 456-8512, info@windplayer.com, www.windplayer.com.

Other music magazines also publish articles on saxophones, sax playing and sax players.

BOOKS

- *The Art of Saxophone Playing*, by Larry Teal (Summy Birchard Inc., New Jersey, USA, 1963. Lots of useful information about saxophones, mouthpieces and reeds, including extensive chapters on adjusting reeds, embouchure, tone quality, breathing technique, intonation, vibrato and more.
- *The Cambridge Companion to the Saxophone* (Cambridge Companions to Music), by Richard Ingham (Editor) (Cambridge University Press, 1999). A comprehensive

guide to the saxophone, its history, technical development and repertoire.

- *Celebrating the Saxophone*, by Paul Lindemeyer (Hearst Books, published by William Morrow & Co., Inc. 1996). A colourful and affectionate look at and a chronological guide and historical tribute to the saxophone, with an accent on the role of the instrument and its influence on pop culture. Many illustrations.

THE INTERNET

The Internet offers plenty of advice and information about saxes, players, reeds, mouthpieces, and much else beside, some of it more valuable than the rest. Here are the URLs (Internet addresses) of a few interesting and reliable Web sites.

- *The International Saxophone Home Page* (ISHP) (www.sax-ophone.org) has loads of tips, FAQs (frequently asked questions) and answers, links to other relevant Web sites, and the *Saxophone Buyer's Guide* by Webmaster Jason DuMars.
- *Bubba's Saxophone Links* offers a lot of useful links at www.mindspring.com/~mgm/saxlinks.html.
- Links can also be found at www.sdam.com/HarmonyMusicList/instr/brass/index.shtm (*The Harmony Music List*) and at *The Music Industry Pages* (www.musicindustry.com).
- To add your own link to a long list of sites, go to members.aol.com/saxring.
- Instrument manufacturers normally have their URL in the form www.[brandname].com, where [brandname] should be replaced by the appropriate brand name.

Newsgroups

Mouthpieces, reeds, instruments, playing techniques and related subjects are discussed in a number of newsgroups, such as rec.music.makers.saxophone, alt.music.makers.woodwind, and alt.music.saxophone, and they are also great places to ask questions – but do read the FAQs first.

Things change

Web sites and newsgroups on the Internet can change address or be renamed pretty frequently. By using search engines, such as Alta Vista or Yahoo, you'll be able to find them at their new location.

ESSENTIAL DATA

In the event of your equipment being stolen or lost, or if you decide to sell it, it's useful to have all relevant data to hand. Here are two pages for those notes. For the insurance company, for the police or just for yourself.

INSURANCE

Company:

Phone: Fax:

Agent:

Phone: Fax:

Policy number:

Premium:

INSTRUMENTS AND ACCESSORIES

Make and model:

Serial number:

Value:

Specifications:

Date of purchase:

Place of purchase:

Phone: Fax:

Make and model:

Serial number:

Value:

Specifications:

Date of purchase:

Place of purchase:

Phone: Fax:

Make and model:

Serial number:

Value:

Specifications:

Date of purchase:

Place of purchase:

Phone: Fax:

ADDITIONAL NOTES

....
....
....
....
....
....
....
....
....
....
....
....
....
....
....
....
....
....
....
....
....
....
....

ROUGH GUIDE
Music Books
Music Reference Guides

Essential CD Guides

Mini Guides

ROUGH GUIDE
Instrument Guides

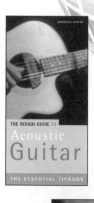

THE ROUGH GUIDE TO
Acoustic Guitar
THE ESSENTIAL TIPBOOK

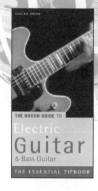

THE ROUGH GUIDE TO
Electric Guitar & Bass Guitar
THE ESSENTIAL TIPBOOK

THE ROUGH GUIDE TO
Piano
THE ESSENTIAL TIPBOOK

THE ROUGH GUIDE TO
Keyboards & Digital Piano
THE ESSENTIAL TIPBOOK

THE ROUGH GUIDE TO
Saxophone
THE ESSENTIAL TIPBOOK

THE ROUGH GUIDE TO
Violin & Viola
THE ESSENTIAL TIPBOOK

ESSENTIAL TIPBOOK
SERIES

Coming in 2001

THE ROUGH GUIDE TO
Clarinet
THE ESSENTIAL TIPBOOK

THE ROUGH GUIDE TO
Flute
THE ESSENTIAL TIPBOOK